MW00709348

BONDAGE

FREEDOM

VICTORY

R. E. Harris

TENNESSEE VALLEY
Publishing®

2006

Library of Congress Control Number: 2006935966

Published by:
Tennessee Valley Publishing
PO Box 52527
Knoxville, Tennessee 37950-2527

Printed and bound in the United States of America.

ISBN 1-932604-40-5

My purpose for writing this book is threefold:

To give hope to those who
have known the pain and fear
of repeated rejection,
low self image, and abuse.

To show those who have experienced
the seeming hopelessness of an addiction
that you can be an over comer.

To answer the question for anyone
trying to work a Twelve Step Program
of Recovery and having no peace:
"Is this all there is?"

My fervent prayer is that by reading this book, many will experience a life changing hope as they have never known. A victorious, joyful life with absolutely no limits, no fears, and a brand new beginning.

A man's greatness

is not measured

by his accomplishments

or riches,

but by what it takes

to discourage him

Contents

Acknowledgments

My Deepest Thanks:
To the **God** I have come to know and love,
To my wife **Bonnie**, who has been an anchor in my life,
To my Godly **Mother**, who prayed faithfully for me,
To my sister, **Sandy**, who greatly assisted me in getting
these words on paper.

To **Jim Smith**, my brother in the Lord, thanks for your
help. And to so many Godly **mentors** who have been a
part of my life. Thanks from the bottom of my heart.

R. E. Harris

PART I
BONDAGE

Chapter 1
A RECIPE FOR PROBLEMS

I was born in a small town on the Eastern Shore of Maryland February 8, 1949. I am the fourth of eight children, five sisters and three brothers. My earliest memories, at approximately age five, was seeing my forty-one year old father sick in bed a lot and his numerous trips to the hospital.

He had suffered rheumatic fever as a child and his now weak heart and damaged heart valves were attributed to that childhood illness. He had undergone open heart surgery at University Hospital in Baltimore, Maryland, which, at the time was a rare and complex procedure.

Prior to this my Dad had been a carpenter and brick mason. My Mom, Dad, two brothers, one sister, and I were living in the house that he had built. He was a very proud man and his inability to provide for his family, due to his illness, had a very negative effect on the entire family.

It seemed to take very little for him to go into a rage. He often took out his frustrations on my brother Bob and I over what seemed, to us, to be very small mistakes. His punishments were unusually brutal and very harsh to say the least. As time went on we were made to feel like objects rather than sons.

Chapter 2
THE WAY I REMEMBER IT

Since we lived in a farming community my brother and I were often hired out to local farmers to clean out stables and chicken houses for thirty five cents an hour to help bring money into the home. During certain harvesting seasons we would stay out of school to pick tomatoes, strawberries, peppers and other crops. We would also spend all day in the soybean fields pulling weeds from between the rows or loading crops out of the field onto wagons.

In summers I recall my older sister Charlotte babysitting my younger sisters under a shade tree all day while we, including my Mom, would pick tomatoes in the scorching sun. On a few occasions my Dad would go behind us and check how well we were picking and if he found a space we had skipped we would be punished severely. I will never forget that large razor strap he used and the bloody marks and welts on my brothers and my legs and backsides.

During the summer on Saturdays we had two cemeteries and some private lawns we had to mow with a push mower. There were hundreds of tombstones that we had to trim around with a pair of scissors on our hands and knees. Sometimes our hands would be covered with blisters and open sores from old broken blisters, but that was no excuse for stopping. All of the money that we made went directly to the household, not to us. I recall never seeing the inside of a movie theater till I was thirteen years old.

Chapter 3
NOT ALL BAD

Needless to say, I have very few fond memories of my childhood. But one fond memory occurred when I was about eight or nine. There was this very cute little blond haired, blue eyed girl who began to visit her grandparents on weekends about two houses down the road. She came all dressed up with pigtails to play with my sisters. She captivated me when I first laid eyes on her. Whenever I got near her I always got this warm feeling inside and always hated to see her leave. I would play with her and my sisters every moment I could.

One time when her Grandmom was calling her home, she gave me a kiss on the cheek and all my brothers and sisters teased me relentlessly, but I didn't care. I remember that I couldn't wait till the next weekend, usually Sunday, to go to her Grandmom's house to see if she had come that day. I was always so disappointed when she didn't. Gradually we started playing together more than she played with my sisters, and I was teased even more, but it didn't seem to matter. Every time she left we always kissed each other on the cheek and said goodbye. At the age of nine I was certain that we were inseparable and I was equally certain that she was the one for me forever.

Chapter 4
UNREQUITED YOUNG LOVE.
REJECTION; NEW INGREDIENTS.

One day I heard my Mom talking to a neighbor about our Elementary school being closed down. All the kids in our town would be attending the school in the next town, which just happened to be the school that my future bride attended. I could not wait for school to start so I would be with her every day. Upon arriving the first day of school, I carefully watched everyone in the halls, waiting to find her. When I finally saw her, much to my surprise, she was walking hand in hand with another boy. They looked like Ken and Barbie. I remember that cold nauseous feeling and at the same time an anger that stirred inside me. That warm feeling with butterflies I had felt was no longer there. At that moment I concluded that I was not good enough for her. They were so well dressed and I had on old worn jeans, a plaid shirt, and worn out shoes.

From that day on whenever I met her in the hall or saw her in the cafeteria, I would get a knot in my stomach and feel nervous. I never spoke to her again although we attended the same Elementary and High schools for the next six years. This was the first of my many deep rejections that I never faced or confronted. I never shared with anyone how deeply hurt I felt.

After my Dad recovered from his surgery, we started attending this small one room church. We would hear the preacher while we were there and on the way home we would hear about what so and so said or did or how the kid's Sunday school teacher would curse like a trained parrot when she got angry. We also heard how our pianist, Henrietta, would be absent because she was in the State Hospital with a nervous breakdown a couple times a year. We also learned that her husband, who was the official greeter, was not above patting the young ladies on the rear while hugging and greeting them. The pastor discovered that I had a good voice and put a young man named Jerry and I together to sing a duet each Sunday along with the choir. After a few months I learned on the way home one Sunday that the duet was going to be cancelled. It seems that Jerry's Grandma, a pillar in the church, had made it clear that she was not going to have her well dressed grandson standing up there beside someone "dressed like a bum." My Dad looked at me and said he wouldn't let me sing with Jerry again if they begged him. So the duet ended.

Chapter 5
ENTERING INTO BONDAGE.
DISCOVERING THE PLEASURES
OF ALCOHOL, FALSE COURAGE.

When I was twelve I started hanging out with a boy named Gary. He was the son of a very successful farmer and always had money in his pocket. We would camp out sometimes in the woods on his farm in a tent. He always knew his Dad would check on us after dark and then we would be free to take off. They had some laborers living in tenant houses a mile or so down the road on one of their other farms. They would always party and drink on the weekends. Gary would plan ahead and give one of them money to buy a six pack of beer or malt liquor and a pint of whiskey. He always had plenty of cigarettes on hand.

I remember the first time I tasted beer and whiskey. It tasted terrible, but I pretended to like it. One thing I didn't have to pretend was the way it made me feel. After a couple of beers and some shots of that liquor I felt ten feet tall. I didn't care what anyone thought about me, nor did I feel inferior to anyone. I remember thinking, "Man, this is the greatest thing in the world."

I discovered that when I was drunk I had the courage to talk to girls and even ask them to dance at the school dances. All the rejections and low self esteem seemed to melt away and I felt like the person I wanted to be. I used to do things while under the influence of alcohol that I didn't remember, but my friends would laugh and tell me about them. I thought it was normal to forget things while drinking and never discussed it with anyone.

On one occasion while hanging out near the movie theater, one of my friends suggested that we walk across the steel pipe railing of the drawbridge spanning the Pocomoke River. This river had very strong churning currents. When you looked down about thirty feet, the water looked very dark and it was moving very swiftly.

I was told that it was approximately fifty to sixty feet deep at the bridge. Many good swimmers had tried to swim across the one hundred yard wide area, only to drown or to be rescued because the undertow was so strong. One or two guys said they were going to "tightrope" walk across the round pipe hand railing to the other side.

We had all been drinking heavily and it was getting late. They dared me to do it also and said I was chicken if I didn't. Although I had never learned to swim, I could not pass up a dare. Even with all the alcohol in me I was still scared stiff, but did not let on to the others. Miraculously I was able to make it all the way across without falling. This was just one of many insane, life threatening things I did while drunk. I now know that someone's hand was upon me.

Chapter 6
EMBARRASSED BY POVERTY,
LOWERING SELF ESTEEM

Well, our family continued to grow, with four younger sisters from the time I was five till fourteen. We kept struggling financially with so many kids. I remember one very embarrassing Christmas; some church people came from the next town to bring us some used toys and clothes. Among those people were two brothers that I went to school with. I tried to turn away to avoid being recognized by them, but they spoke to me and I was very ashamed. I tried to avoid them in school after that. I was very embarrassed of my clothes and sometimes my shoes would come apart at the toe and my socks would stick out.

Kids can sometimes be very cruel about the things you wear and those comments just confirmed in my own mind that I was not as good as anyone else.

Chapter 7
ADDING TO THE RECIPE

Whenever my brother and I went anywhere, my Dad forbid us to hitchhike, but we did it anyway. Usually when we hitchhiked, we would simply stand on one of the corners of town and stick out our thumb for a ride. I was now thirteen. There was one gentleman whose Dad owned the poultry processing plant in town. He drove a sharp Corvette and always dressed well.

One evening I was trying to thumb a ride to Ocean city when he pulled up to the intersection and offered me a ride. When I got into the car, he asked where I was headed and I told him. He said he was going there also, but had to stop at home and have dinner with his parents, as it was his routine every evening. We had only traveled four or five miles when he asked if I would like a beer or something. I said sure, so he stopped at a convenience store and bought a six pack. I drank a couple on the way to Salisbury before we arrived at his very exquisite condo next to the city park. His Mom and Dad's condo was not far from his.

He asked me if I wanted a drink while I waited for him to go to dinner at his parent's. He made me a whiskey sour and I watched TV until he returned. It never occurred to me to ask myself why someone so cool and prosperous would want to hang out with me, although I thought of myself as being much more mature than my age.

When he returned, we proceeded to head to Ocean City and cruised the strip hoping to find some dates. I was convinced that it would be pretty easy, while riding around in a red Corvette convertible. I continued to consume a few more beers while cruising. Around ten o'clock we had kind of given up on picking up dates. He suggested that since he had to go to work the next morning and I also had to head back home, that I crash on his couch for the night. I didn't see any problem with that and I thanked him. When we arrived at his condo he made me another drink and turned on the TV. The next thing I remember is feeling like I was in a trance, partially asleep, yet still awake, and he was sexually molesting me. I thought it was just a bad dream as I was unable to resist or put up a fight against him. I'd had no idea that he had slipped something in my drink.

When I awoke enough to get my thoughts together, I realized that I was mostly nude and sensed that I had been violated. I got myself dressed, although I felt very dizzy and weak, and got out of there as fast as I could. I remember feeling the shame and embarrassment and never mentioned this incident to another person on earth.

In the next few years I had such hatred toward homosexuals. I took my anger out on them in a physical way. As a result of all my physical hard work, I had become quite muscular, and I was confident that I could take on anybody in a fight and beat him. I would pretend to be friendly with a homosexual, go for a ride with him, and wind up beating him, and stealing his money, booze and car, leaving him alongside the road. I hated them all.

Chapter 8
FINDING MY NICHE

Along with my treatment of gays, and my sometimes violent insane behavior, I was accepted by a couple of older boys to hang out with. At least one of my older friends was always able to buy alcohol for us as we hung out. I grew to trust absolutely no one for anything.

By now my brother and I were hooking school a lot and hanging out at the pool halls. We were always careful to get home at the same time as if coming home from school. We were both smoking regularly, though never near our parents or other family members.

There was another family that lived about three miles from us. They had four sons that attended school with us. My father had forbidden us to ever go to their home because the parents drank heavily every weekend. We would still go over there every chance we could, but would claim to be going somewhere else. The reason we liked going there was that the parents would give us cigarettes and beer whenever we wanted and if they passed out we would take one of their bottles of liquor and take off.

My life was beginning to be full of rebellion as well as a quest for more and more alcohol to reinforce my feeling about life.

My brother and I joined the Boy Scout Troop in our small town. We would go camping once a month at the same place. Some of us would plan ahead and hide some beer and liquor down at the sandpit near our campsite. After the scout leader was asleep, we would sneak off and party till late. He always wondered why we were so reluctant to get up in the morning.

Chapter 9
MIXED EMOTIONS

When I was about fourteen years old, my Dad's health began to gradually decline. It was determined that he would have to undergo another open heart surgery. He always did all the driving for the family as my Mom had never driven or learned how. My brother and I would be asked to drive at certain times, when two or more vehicles were required. We had lots of experience at driving farm equipment, pickups and farm trucks on the road. Our town was approximately one hundred and fifty miles from Baltimore, but the bus station was only thirty minutes from us.

On the day my father was scheduled to go in for surgery, he drove Mom and me to the station and I was to drive back home, even though I had no license yet. As he took his suitcase and we were saying our goodbyes, he shook my hand for the very first time and said "Be a big help to Mom while I am gone." I had a very strange feeling when he shook my hand and looked me in the eyes. I could never remember my Dad hugging me or shaking my hand at any time.

Mom and I had a quiet ride home, I could tell that she was worried. About three or four days later, on Sunday morning, Mom and I drove to the bus station

17

to make the trip to Baltimore. I remember that she had a big bag with extra clothes for Dad and I was carrying a portable TV for his room. Mom had received word that he was through surgery and in ICU recovering.

Upon arriving at the Baltimore bus station, we walked the five or six blocks to University Hospital because we could not afford a cab. When we arrived at the hospital I sat down in a waiting room, resting from carrying the TV so far. Mom went to get information as to where Dad was in recovery.

After a few minutes she came back sobbing loudly and was being helped by two assistant nurses to a chair next to me. I asked what was wrong. The nurses couldn't look at me so I sensed something was wrong. When Mom could finally speak she said "Dad is gone." I asked "What did you say?" She said Dad had died about an hour before we had arrived. I remember feeling a numbness and a feeling of disbelief. I never cried or showed any emotion, I tried to comfort Mom. She wanted to go see him for the last time, but they said that would not be wise because he had not been cleaned up after the surgery and she would not want to remember him that way.

After some discussions with the doctors, signing some papers, and making arrangements for his body to be taken back home, we proceeded quietly back to the bus station. On the long bus ride home Mom met a girl from our home town who had been visiting a friend for the weekend and was on her way home. She sat in the seat next to Mom all the way home and tried to comfort her. She was one grade ahead of me in school but we knew each other casually. I chose a seat behind Mom and just sat silently. The girl looked back at me and asked if I was alright. I responded yes. I sat there staring out the window feeling both sad and almost relieved at the same time.

I recall feeling extremely guilty for a lack of grief and not feeling like crying. I was to carry this guilt for a long time.

Chapter 10
REJECTION

When we got home we had to contact all the relatives and friends and even my older brother and sister who were married by now and not living at home. We lived in a very old creaky dark house across from a cemetery and I remember being terrified of closing my eyes at night and trying to fall asleep with all the strange noises. We had learned after buying the house that an old couple had died in one of the downstairs bedrooms and everyone said it was haunted.

On the day of Dad's funeral at least two or three people looked at me and said "Now you're going to have to be the man of the house." I was terrified of that thought, as I had four younger sisters. Even so, I still felt a responsibility to see to the safety and care of the younger ones. The one thing that used to break my heart was when my next to the youngest sister, Sandy, would look at me and ask when her Daddy was coming home. I didn't know what to say and would try so hard to change the subject as if I didn't hear her question. I truly felt that this Loving God that I heard about in Sunday school either did not exist or did not care about us at all. I was so scared of living in that house at night.

I became like a lot of people, thinking I knew about God and how He did things, but not knowing anything about Him really. Of course I didn't bother to try to find out either.

The funeral came and went and all the people left except for one of Dad's sisters and a few close relatives. As I look back now, of all the men in our church, not one of them ever came by to talk to me or ask if I wanted to go hunting or fishing, or just to ask me how I was or to pray with me. Later when I got into some trouble at age fifteen, word got back to me that a couple of the men were discussing my situation and one of them commented that they should lock him up and throw away the key. These were the same farmers and pillars of the church that worked me in the fields and stables for thirty-five cents an hour. They never tried to talk to me or mentor me. I had so many resentments in my life already that I just added them to the list.

Chapter 11
REBELLION AND THE RESULT

I discovered that if I had a few beers or a couple of gulps of whiskey at night, I could go to sleep and not be nearly as afraid. We had an old pump house building behind the house because we had a well, not city water. I used to keep some malt liquor and whiskey hidden behind some old boxes out there. In the evenings I would often pretend to go for a walk or just sit outside, but in reality, I was in the pump house getting enough in me to see the girls to bed and put myself to bed and actually go to sleep.

My Dad's grave was in the cemetery right across the street, but I never visited it. I began to use alcohol a lot when more courage was required for anything. Within a few months of my father's death, two of my friends and I broke into the small grocery store down the road, which was owned by the husband of the church grandmother that previously broke up our duet.

She was a pillar in the church, but he never attended. We stole cigarettes, snacks, a jar of coins and some other petty things. We hid them under the foundation of my house and would go help ourselves whenever we wanted.

A couple of weeks later I was with the same friends in the next town where we hung out on the street and in front of the movie theater. I was very intoxicated and one of us came up with the idea of breaking into the bowling alley after it closed. The younger of my two friends had a sister who worked there. She told him that they left cash there at night. We waited till about one o'clock in the morning and broke a back door glass and made off with quite a bit of cash. Well that was Friday night. The next day the younger of the two friends, who was thirteen, began to flash around a lot of big currency and was brought in for questioning at the police station. He told them everything and the next thing I knew the police were at my house with a warrant and hauled me off to jail. I stayed in jail for about three months awaiting a trial. I'll never forget the look of disappointment and hurt on my Mom's face when she came to visit me behind bars the first time. I didn't even want to face her because she was crying and asked me "Why?"

I just acted like I was cool and that it didn't bother me because the other inmates were all there too. I just stuffed the feelings, along with all the rest of them, inside me.

I had quit school about a month before my arrest and the judge gave me a choice. I was to either return to school or go to prison. Needless to say, I chose school.

The day I got home from jail my Mom sent me to the store that we had broken into. She gave me ten dollars, which was a lot to her, and said "Give this to the store owner along with my deepest apologies." I was also to tell him that I would make restitution in weekly payments till the debt was settled. Mom was a very honest person and told me that this was the first step in making things right. When I walked into the store I laid the money on the counter and began to apologize and do as Mom had told me. Before I got a couple of words out, he threw the money in my face and said that he didn't want my kind of trash in his store and to never return. He cursed at me the whole way out of the store.

The principal at my school didn't want me back there because he was more than a little tired of my behavior. My probation officer convinced the principal of another school in the county to try me out for a period of time. I won't forget our first meeting, or screening if you will. He was a small, soft spoken person and I guess he wanted to get his point across that there would be no misbehavior of any kind. As my probation officer and I were escorted to the back

Rebel at age 15.

office, I looked around the table and it looked liked a luncheon for the Green Bay Packers.

The principal had arranged to have his very large vice principal, head coach, assistant coach, industrial arts teacher and another very large teacher present for this interview. I was told in no uncertain terms the conditions of my attending this school and I very politely agreed to them. I never blended in with the crowd too well with my black boots, blue jeans, tight t-shirts and denim vest. This quickly got the attention of the school bully, who had broken a few arms and seemed to have everyone intimidated by his size, strength, and reputation. Pete was a very large farm boy. I think he bench pressed a few cows before going to school in the morning. I was the only one who gave him a challenge at arm wrestling on the desk, though I can't recall ever winning a match. I tried to avoid him as best I could because I knew I was treading on thin ice already with the authorities.

Chapter 12
HOW TO MESS UP A GOOD THING

The industrial arts teacher, Mr. Dolby, seemed to take a liking to me after a while. We would do woodworking, welding and even fix lawnmowers in the shop. While he was teaching the class, I would quite often sneak into the welding room (it had an exhaust fan) and smoke a cigarette. He noticed a gift in me for mechanical work. I could tear down an old lawnmower that wouldn't run and soon have it together and purring away. Mr. Dolby would encourage me to focus on that talent. He would sometimes write a permission slip for me to miss a certain class to work in the shop.

One of my school friends had a pickup truck and Mr. Dolby would often send three of us for supplies and materials for building picnic benches and other projects. Sometimes on the very nice days we would be out drinking beer and going to the beach, only to return just before school let out. He let us slide a lot on our trips. I began to work on his vehicles and other friends' vehicles in the shop. I never had a car or license while in school. This didn't help my self esteem at all, but others always bragged about my mechanical abilities.

Mr. Dolby would later help me land my first job as an apprentice mechanic at a GM dealership. The owner was a close friend of his. My assignments at first were just to clean up the tools and floors and to wash parts for the techs. Later they trained me to work a lift, change oil, undercoat cars and to perform a pre-delivery inspection on new vehicles. I would work after school and half-a-day on Saturday. I really admired some of those techs who were so good at diagnosing problems; especially the one who built the performance cars.

As a part of the new vehicle inspection, they all had to be road tested for noises and proper handling. My employer had never asked me if I had a license and I never volunteered the fact that I didn't.

I usually road tested down a side road by the dealership and not on the main highway. I sometimes would skip school once or twice a month and work.

On one particular day I had just completed checking over a new Corvette high performance model. I had to road test it and decided to drive it to school since it was lunch time and I knew some of my friends would be out in the parking lot smoking, as usual. When I arrived, several of them gathered around the car admiring it and wishing they were behind the wheel. Man, I felt like I was really cool sitting there in that Vette with the engine sounding real tough. Soon a guy named Dicky Lee walked over and asked me if I wanted to run him in his high performance Ford. Some of my friends said, "Yeah Ron, go out and take him." I was on such an ego trip by now, I said, "Sure, why not."

We paired off right in front of the school and lit them up right there. Well I spanked him pretty good and my big head and I went back to work. Little did I know that the principal found out who was burning up the road in that new Vette and called my boss. When I walked back to the service department to hang up the keys, my service manager reached out for the keys and informed me that my services were no longer need there. All my coworkers had a big laugh and cracked a few jokes as I was on my way out. It hurt me because some of these guys really acted like they were my friends while I was there.

On Monday morning I was called into the principal's office for an even bigger surprise. He suspended me for a week and had called my probation officer to inform him of my behavior. When I got home I called my probation officer with many apologies and informed him of my actions and the consequences. I acted like I didn't know that the principal had already told him so I that I would appear to be honest, sincere and forthcoming. After a short lecture, he told me to spend my time off from school seeking other part-time employment, which I did.

Mr. Dolby came through for me again. He spoke to another of his friends who happened to be the owner of the local Ford dealership. He didn't mention the Vette incident or that I had ever worked at the other place.

I went over to fill out an employment application as the owner had suggested and I was hired shortly thereafter. I didn't put down the other place as a reference and I never took anymore cars to school again!

Chapter 13
CHARMED BY A SMILE

Things were finally starting to get back to normal with school and work. I started noticing a cute little girl I'd met in the hall at school. She would always give me a shy little smile and when I turned to look at her she was sometimes looking back.

Occasionally I'd see her by the lockers with a girlfriend. She would smile at me and then turn and whisper to her friend. She was never dressed real fine or fancy, nor was her friend, whom she was often with.

One day in the cafeteria, I finally found the courage to ask her name. She was one grade behind me, I was currently a junior. I discovered that she had a brother in my class and was one of seven kids. I later found out that her family was about as poor as mine was.

One Saturday night, not long after meeting her, I was hanging out with a couple of friends in front of the movie theater. I saw her walking towards the theater and she had to pass right by me. As usual, she gave me that shy little smile. My friends and I had been drinking some beer earlier and I guess I had just enough false courage to go over and ask her if she was going to see the show. When she replied yes, I asked if I could sit with her and she shyly said "Yeah, sure." I don't remember what the movie was, but it sure seemed to end too soon for me. I walked her out front and said "I'll see you at school on Monday" and she said "See you then."

I eventually started walking her to class sometimes and I remember that warm butterfly feeling in my stomach whenever I was near her. On the weekends we started meeting at the movies. I was so happy when I was with her.

Chapter 14
TROUBLE ALWAYS SEEMS TO FIND YOU

One day after a long period of avoiding any conflict with the school bully, he cornered me by the lockers and dared me to go outside to fight. There were about three of my classmates present and they looked at me to see what my response would be.

I knew there were three choices I could make. I could chicken out and lose the respect of all my classmates who were beginning to look up to me. Second, would be to beat him real bad with any means I could to equalize myself with him, and go back to jail. Thirdly, I could go out there and let him beat me to a pulp and still save face by not being a chicken.

I tried to convince him that my going out there would probably lead to my suspension and jail time. His response was that he thought I was a coward and scared of him. With that comment said, I told him to lead the way and we would get it on.

I guess since no one else would ever call him out, some of the classmates began to spread the chatter all through the hall and came following behind us down the long corridor. Before we hit the door there was quite an audience.

Well, I had learned on the streets and in jail that you don't wait for your enemy to strike first. As soon as he was through the door I laid a couple of real good blows on him along with a couple of good hard kicks.

He was much larger and stronger than I, so I knew I had to keep laying blows to the face and quickly withdraw before he could get a hold of me. The only problem with my formula was that the blows were not having the normal results that I was used to seeing. I only had to make one mistake, and that was not moving fast enough, he got a good crack at me and I went down. Before I could regain my composure he was on top of me landing some blows.

About this time three very large seniors grabbed him and pulled him off me, then two other seniors held me back so that we couldn't get to each other. We were both escorted to the office and put in separate rooms, licking our wounds. The principal had the seniors stay with each of us during our discussion.

We were both suspended for three days and my probation officer was informed again by the principal. I was certain that this was the final straw after he called and arranged a meeting. After explaining the position I had been placed in and the well known reputation of the bully injuring other kids during other confrontations, my officer told me that I needed to walk a straight line from here on. He then smiled and said "at least you chose the biggest one of the bunch to mess with." I'll never forget my officer, Jack L., for his patience, understanding and mercy.

Chapter 15
ALWAYS JUST OUT OF REACH

Well, after my suspension was over I resumed school as usual, walking my sweetheart to class. Word got back to her parents that she was seeing me and they forbid her to ever see me again. I think one of her sisters or brothers mentioned it or let it slip out, but her parents had previously read about my arrest in the paper. They told her that I was a nobody and a trouble maker. We continued to walk to classes but we had to sneak around every chance we could get on the weekends because if her younger siblings saw us together they would probably tell on her unless she bribed them.

By now I was seventeen and she was fifteen. Since grade school, I never thought that I could feel like this around anyone. We took many risks to meet at her cousin's house or at the drive-in or a dance. I just knew she was the one for me. She remained a virgin all of the three years we were together and many of our friends were not. I continued my drinking even while going with her.

Now I was a senior and my drinking was escalating. Our many trips, from shop class to the beach or anywhere else we could drink, continued. One night I was with three or four others and I had drank till I passed out on the back seat. I had not eaten anything and had been drinking all that Saturday. I guess one of them had the idea to break into a service station and steal tools and money. They were caught a couple of days later and I was implicated along with them. So here I was back in jail again and calling my probation officer explaining that I was out cold and didn't even know anything about this caper.

This was the first time that anyone ever hinted or suggested that just maybe I had a drinking problem. I thought it was ridiculous but I had to admit that most of the times I did bad things or was exposed to bad incidents, it had something to do with drinking.

Well, Jack L. went to bat for me again with the judge, convincing him that I was truly not involved in this one. After my name hit the paper again, my girlfriend's parents became more convinced of how worthless I was. In fact, her father threatened to shoot me on sight if I ever came on his property. We continued sneaking around their backs somehow or another.

There was this boy named Billy Joe that was the eldest son of the family our parents forbid us to visit or play with because of his parents' drinking and bizarre behavior. He and I hung out and drank together when we were younger. He had joined the

Marines and went to Vietnam. While he was there he was wounded and sent home. Soon after his return home he was driving a nice new sporty Chevelle. My girlfriend's parents seemed bent on getting her to go out with him. They didn't know his background or his parents. All they knew was that he was a war hero, had a nice car and seemed to be going places. In fact, they said that if she were going to go out with anyone, it would be Billy Joe.

Billy Joe and I went from being friends to being worst enemies. I even parked at the end of her father's long driveway one night daring him to come out there after he took her home. He got the word and stayed in the house like a coward. I finally left. It was never the same with us after he came into the scene, but she still would sneak out to see me and we would spend hours together talking. I really trusted that she wouldn't allow her parents to pressure her into choosing Billy Joe over me.

One afternoon my brother came home while I was working on an old car at the house. He asked me "Have you heard the news?" I said, "What news?" He proceeded to tell me that she and Billy Joe had gotten married yesterday. He went into the house and I went and sat in the pump house and started to cry. I had that old sinking, nauseous feeling in my gut again. I started drinking and tried to forget and whenever anyone would mention her, I would act like it didn't bother me, even though I felt that I was dying inside.

She even contacted me to meet her with one of her girlfriends and I did. She was crying and saying how sorry she was, that she had made a big mistake. She said that she just wanted to get out of that old run down rental farmhouse with little food, old clothes and six siblings. She saw no other way out. Then she kissed me and I said "See ya," as if I didn't care. I went off alone and drank myself drunk. I began to drink even more now that I had lost her. I can look back and see that I had also lost the ability or willingness to show anything but anger. I would get into fights at the drop of a hat. I was building my fortress so that no one could ever hurt me like that again.

Chapter 16
GRADUATION CELEBRATION

Icontinued on in my senior year, skipping lots of classes, with permission slips from Mr. Dolby. Our party trips continued as well. One of my friends, Bill, who often went on our school time trips, had a girlfriend at our school. She was about three years younger than him. Almost every time we would meet in the hallway, she would be winking and flirting at me behind his back. She had a reputation of being, shall we say, "loose." She relentlessly continued this pursuit of me and sometimes I think Bill suspected it. She was only fifteen. I was about nineteen now because I turned eighteen in my junior year. Some time lapsed after I had quit school and I had to redo my sophomore year.

I remembered that my lost love didn't like this girl at all and had spoken of her many times when she would see her with Bill in the hall. She called her a tramp and some other choice names. She was not an unattractive girl by far, but she was not what I would consider beautiful either. I never paid much attention to her advances or asked her out.

I continued drinking and hanging out throughout the rest if my senior year. On the night before graduation I hitchhiked to Salisbury and began drinking heavily. At about eleven p.m. I went into the bus station and sat in a booth. I ordered something to eat but by the time the food got there I had passed out or fell asleep. I guess the waitress called the local police when I could not be awakened. The only thing I remember is someone grabbing me and dragging me out very abruptly. My normal response kicked in and I turned on the one I thought was attacking me. Little did I know he was a police officer and he had a partner who had no intention of being a bystander. The next thing I know I was cuffed and thrown into the back of a cruiser. Then I was booked and put into the drunk tank to sleep it off.

The next morning I awoke on a steel bunk with no mattress and couldn't remember why I was there. I called my Mom at work to let her know I was okay and told her where I was. That evening I was to attend my graduation ceremony. My mother had so looked forward to this day because none of my older siblings had been able to finish school and graduate.

She worked at a nursing home owned by Mrs. Holland who was a very kind and giving person. In fact, I used to do the mowing and gardening for her at her home and the nursing home. When she saw the distressed look on my Mom's face she asked her what was wrong. My Mom explained the dilemma and Mrs. Holland drove her to Salisbury. Mrs.

Holland, bless her heart, put up the bail so my Mother could see me get my diploma that night. I knew my name was in the paper again and some of my classmates were sure to read it. I began drinking that afternoon right up to the time of the ceremony so that I would have the courage to face everyone and walk up on stage to receive my diploma. I graduated and went on to work at the Ford dealership full time. I also began a relationship with the girl who used to flirt with me. Shortly thereafter we became engaged.

Chapter 17
FAST CARS FOR FAST TIMES

It wasn't long before I bought a used car that had been traded in by the father of two boys. He said it was too much for them to handle and decided to get them something with a lot less power. It was a '66 Chevelle SS 396 and had been boosted up even beyond the factory horsepower. The first couple of times I drove it I was a little scared of it. This thing was like a rocket engine in an orange crate! It would pin you back so hard in the seat when you punched it that a grown man could not pull himself forward toward the dash with all his strength.

One night in particular I recall having a few beers and decided I was going to show a few buddies just what it would do. I popped the clutch and burned out. When I hit second gear the whole dash and car would slam and shake. When I hit third gear I suddenly heard a loud roaring of the engine almost like an explosion that was followed by what sounded like a screaming chainsaw wide open. I immediately shut it down and coasted to the side of the road. My friend lived about two miles away and some of them went to get his truck to tow me over to his workshop at his farm.

The next day when I started examining the damage I discovered that under the severe torque, the clutch and flywheel had broken loose and sawed through the cast iron flywheel housing and over halfway through the floorboard just before deflecting down onto the road. In fact, we went back to where it had happened later and there were parts of the sharp jagged metal imbedded into the road. The opening to the left side of the floorboard looked like someone had taken a very large skill saw to it or ripped it with a chainsaw. This opening was about three inches from my right leg.

There was a man named John who ran a speed and custom shop in Salisbury. He'd had the same experience on the drag strip a couple of years earlier. His flywheel did come through and severed his leg between the ankle and knee. Not long after that, the drag strip authorities passed a law that any vehicle exceeding a certain amount of horsepower had to have a special hardened flywheel housing and a reinforced blow proof floorboard. I didn't truly realize how fortunate and blessed I was.

It took me a few weeks to get enough parts to put the rocket back on the road. By the way, I still had not gotten my license yet and the tag that I had was usually stolen from another car. I would occasionally get liquored up and drive downtown by the movie theater. When I saw a local city police car I would light it up at the stoplight just to see him come after me. Those city police cars didn't really have much muscle, but it was fun watching them fade in the distance. Once in a while they would radio out to the state boys to set up a road block on Route 13, but I would take to a side road or field, if necessary, to evade them. I used to say "They can't take my license because I don't have one."

One evening I was on a double date with my sister Linda and her boyfriend. While we were at the drive-in, where we hung out, we saw a friend who had a '68 Plymouth Roadrunner. He thought he had done enough to it to give me a run. We paired off out on Route 13, a four lane highway, and turned them loose burning rubber and jamming gears. Well, I pulled away from him pretty good in the ¼ mile, but he insisted we go ahead and stretch them out a bit.

I was probably doing 140 mph or better when we passed a boat repair shop. Who could have guessed that there would be two state boys in separate cars having a quiet conversation? I saw them throwing gravel and smoking tires in my rearview mirror, as they started to chase us. My buddy pulled over as one of them threw his lights on him. The other one was coming on strong, but I had no intentions of stopping or letting him catch me. As I approached the GM dealership I immediately flipped the switch on the dash that killed my rear lights so that he couldn't see me braking. I skidded sideways onto the side road by the GM place nearly wiping out three cars in the corner lot by inches. I jammed it into first gear and slammed second and could see the flashing light at the corner that we had just made. As I hit third gear I could see his headlights coming my way. I killed the lights, luckily there was a little bit of moonlight that night. When I hit fourth gear I could see that he was fading back a little.

I knew this road and every curve and bump on it. I don't think the officer knew it as well and he was a little more sane than I. He continued his pursuit for about five miles, around many sharp curves. I finally locked down the brakes and pulled onto a dirt road next to a church in a wooded area. We sat and waited for about half a minute and he went screaming past the dirt road. I was running Mickey Thompson Cheater Slicks with only about ten psi which gave me quite an advantage over the officer, hugging those curves.

Well, I popped a beer and we sat there in the dark until we figured he was long gone. My sister and her date started whining about how bad their hips were hurting and their skinned elbows. The next day their hips were bruised from sliding from one side of the seat to the other and slamming into the side arm rests. They said they never wanted to ride with me again and I think they meant it. In fact, it got harder and harder to find people who would ride with me.

Chapter 18
CARS, A SOURCE OF PLEASURE,
A SOURCE OF SORROW

A few weeks later I asked to borrow my Mom's car on Friday night since mine was broken down again. She reluctantly said yes. I picked up a couple of friends and we started drinking. The next thing I knew I had passed out behind the wheel on the way home at about three a.m. The car went into the woods and smashed into a very large oak tree. The entire front of the car was pushed back to the windshield. I walked away with some facial cuts and some bruises. The corner of the open ashtray in the had cut a large hole less than a half inch from my right eye but I never went to the doctor or got stitches.

I finally made it home just as my Mom was getting up to go to work at six a.m. She had to call a coworker to get a ride to work. Later that day I had a friend with a tow truck bring the car to the house. The only reason the police didn't discover the wreck was because the car had gone so far into the woods. It was difficult to see from the highway. Again I escaped a ticket for driving without a license, let alone serious injuries. I eventually got my license after getting off probation.

One evening when my car was broken down, my brother Bob and I asked my cousin Larry if we could borrow his car to go out. He had to work that night so he said it was okay. As we began drinking we went to several places and then decided that we would go to Salisbury and cruise the strip there. I had been drinking all afternoon and hadn't eaten anything. I found myself drifting off the shoulder of the road a couple of times.

My brother, whose license was currently revoked, suggested that he drive before I killed us both. I stopped and got into the passenger seat and let him drive. He had only been driving about twenty minutes when there were flashing lights behind us. Apparently he was observed weaving and was pulled over. I quickly reached into my wallet and gave him my license. When the officer became suspicious he asked my brother his date of birth. He couldn't answer and confessed that it was my license. We were both cuffed and locked up in the Salisbury jail. Meanwhile, the next morning, my cousin had to go get his impounded car so that he could get to work that evening. I wound up having my license revoked for loaning it to my brother.

We had a friend whose uncle owned a salvage yard. We were able to get another complete front end from another car that matched my Mom's wrecked car at a very low price. It took us about two weeks to transfer all the parts over and have a place straighten the frame underneath. We were able to get her back on the road and she didn't loan it to me anymore.

After working at the Ford dealership for about two years I was able to purchase a brand new '70 Mercury Cyclone GT. I was able to get bank financing and got the car for one hundred dollars over cost as an employee. It was a pretty fast car but not as fast as the Chevelle. I had blown the engine in the Chevelle and sold it to my brother to fix up.

Things were going pretty good at work till one day, about a month after buying the Cyclone, two officers in plain clothes walked into the shop. They asked me to come outside and speak with them. They walked me over to their car and the next thing I knew I was cuffed in the back seat and they were driving me to an unknown location. They didn't respond to any of my questions such as where we were going and why. I was not given a chance to put away any of my tools or lock my tool cabinets or my car sitting out in the parking lot. We finally arrived at the police station in the next county and I was escorted to a private room for questioning. I was informed that I was implicated in a breaking and entering incident by one of my so called friends named Jr. He claimed that I had accompanied and assisted in the robbery of a small store a couple of weeks prior. This same Jr. had been arrested on other charges. One of which was getting drunk and drugged up one Saturday, locking himself and his Mother in a bedroom with a gun to her head and threatening to kill her. After the SWAT team and other authorities showed up in our quiet little town for about thirty minutes, he surrendered to them without anyone being hurt. This was to be one of two similar incidents. This same Jr. was the eldest son of the family my Father had forbidden us to associate with. I think he was a few fries short of a Happy Meal™, but we did occasionally party together.

Getting back to the incident I was being questioned for, I was held and questioned for the next seventy-two hours before being released. I can honestly say that I had nothing to do with that robbery at all.

During my seventy-two hours in custody, I discovered that my younger sister, Linda, who had recently gotten her license, had gone to the dealership where I worked and borrowed my car for a little while. She used the extra set of keys that I always kept at home. Apparently on her way to pick up a friend, she pulled out in front of an oncoming vehicle and my car was hit broadside on the passenger's side. The damage was so severe that had it been hit on the driver's side, she could have been killed. My car was towed to a body shop near the town where the accident occurred.

Upon my release, I was not taken back to where I was picked up by the officers. In fact, I was not given a ride to any destination. I hitchhiked home and got ready for work the next day. When I arrived at work I was politely told that my services were no longer needed there. There had been a rumor spread throughout the shop that I may have been picked up on drug charges since the officers who picked me up were plainclothes. My employer was currently running for County Commissioner and wanted to avoid any and all embarrassment, so whether I was guilty or not made very little difference to him.

Four days before I had a nice job and a beautiful brand new car. Now I had neither. It would be six to seven weeks before I saw my car repaired. When it was finished it looked as if high school students had fixed it. It pulled while driving and wore tires badly. The body work was also terrible. You could see the roughness down the side and the paint was rough. The car was never the same again. When I complained to the body shop they said that I could leave it for another three weeks and they could probably do it better, although they thought it looked fine.

Chapter 19
TRUCKS, A NEW LOVE,
ANOTHER INGREDIENT FOR TROUBLE

It took me a while to land another job especially since I didn't have transportation and my record was not that good at holding a job. I finally went to work at a small service station. The owner had six or seven tractor-trailers. During the week I would pump gas, change oil and maybe an occasional tire. On the weekends some of the big rigs would be back in and would require servicing of the refrigeration unit engines on the trailers. We would also service the large diesel engines and drive trains on the semi tractors. I was very captivated by the size of these engines and the rigs themselves. I got to move them around and park them in the yard out back. It seemed like I was on top of the world sitting in the seat of one of those things. I really wished I could go on a trip with one of them.

It wouldn't be long before I got my wish. Things were a little slow around the station one week and my boss told me I could go on a trip with a driver named Daris B. I was thrilled to go, especially since I knew Daris and had drank with him and some of the other guys there. We had gone about three hundred miles from home headed for Rochester, New York when Daris stopped to fuel up. When we got ready to go he said "It's your turn to drive now." I was terrified at the thought of meeting other vehicles on a two lane road. To make things worse, it had been snowing for about an hour and we were just coming into some serious hills northwest of Harrisburg, Pennsylvania. Nonetheless, I got behind the wheel and he hopped up into the passenger's seat. He watched me for awhile to see if I could stay on the road. He warned me to never let the right front tire go off the side of the road or it would be over for us. He continued to watch me shift that thirteen speed transmission and said that I looked like a pro. Little did he know just how scared I was, especially since I hadn't had any alcohol to help me. After a short time he broke out a bottle of vodka and started hitting it and popping some kind of pills. The next thing I knew he jumped back into the sleeper and said "Keep on truckin."

We made it to Rochester after driving all night in the ice and snow. We were two hours late for the delivery and the owner of the company was not happy at all. He had hired three or four men to be there at six a.m. to unload refrigerated chicken to distribute to his area supermarkets. He had to pay them by the hour whether they were standing around or working. He was furious with us. Daris didn't seem to care too much, since he had spent most of the night drinking vodka and popping pills.

After we were unloaded we had to go pick up another load, which was about one hundred twenty miles from where we were. On the way I told Daris that I was getting sleepy and couldn't keep my eyes open. He handed me two little round green pills and said "Take these and you'll feel fine." He was right. After about an hour and two cups of coffee I felt like I could take on the world. I had never taken any speed or uppers as they called them, but soon discovered that I liked them. Daris hooked me up with his source and I began to use them when I made some trips alone. I could load out of Homestead or Florida City and run all the way to Niagara Falls with only coffee and fuel stops. I couldn't eat while taking the pills but I could be up for days. I recall on one occasion I found myself talking to someone in the passenger's seat, but no one was there. Between the pills and sleep deprivation I started experiencing hallucinations.

I always liked the run up to Niagara because trucks from the States couldn't haul in Canada. I had to drop off my trailer just across the border and lay over for two or three days in a motel in Niagara, Canada. I would always stop taking the pills hours prior to arriving in Canada and then start drinking liquor while staying over. I would drink, party and sleep for three days then sober up before getting behind the wheel again. I was always afraid to drink while driving the rig because I knew that I could accidentally kill a family. Besides, unlike Daris, the pills and alcohol together never agreed with me. One seemed to defeat the other.

On more than one occasion, the NY State Police would stop me and ransack my entire cab and sleeper looking for drugs or weapons. I got smart early and started keeping my pills in a sealed plastic zipper bag behind one of the headlights. They never found any on me and they never put anything back in order after turning my truck inside out. I could never quite figure out why they always picked on me for shakedown, but later after looking at my old license photo I realized that I looked like Charles Manson.

Chapter 20
A BRUSH WITH DEATH

I drove over the road for quite sometime without any real problems. That was probably due to the fact that when I was driving a big semi I never drank or used drugs, because I was afraid of what might happen if I were not alert or in control of myself. The ironic thing was after all my drinking and drug use, the worst accident I ever had was when I was sober.

In June of 1971 I had loaded out of a small town called Cuba, NY. It is located toward the Southwestern end of the state. I was to make one drop in Pittsburgh, PA. and then a drop in Arlington, VA. I was on Route 68, a two lane, very winding steep road. Suddenly as I was coming down an extremely steep grade, my low air pressure warning buzzer sounded. I looked at the pressure gauge and it was very low. I hit my brake pedal to slow the rig, but it had no effect on my speed. I immediately revved the engine and geared down as low as I could, which was eighth gear. I waited to see if my air would build up, but it didn't.

My heart was pounding as the eighty thousand pound rig just kept picking up speed. I knew that at the bottom of this long grade there was a stop sign and you had to go right or left. Straight through the stop sign meant going off a pretty high cliff into the East Brady River and as I could not swim that was not an option. The only option I could think of was to slowly ride over to the right into a sloped rocky wall, hoping to lay the rig down on it's side and slide to a stop. Just as the rig was about to go over, it hit a more vertical rock formation then veered off the left side of the roadway. The last thing I could see was trees coming at me from all directions.

I was momentarily knocked unconscious while the rig plowed a downward path sheering off fully mature trees and everything in it's path. When it finally came to a stop the cab portion that I was trapped in had separated from the chassis. The front axle, engine and transmission had also been severed from the chassis. The fifth wheel that connected the tractor to the trailer was sheered off the tractor and remained with the trailer, which had wrapped around a very large tree. One of the tractor's wheel and tire assemblies had broken loose with such force that it went right through the side of a house nearby. I was later told by one of the attending nurses at the hospital that she heard the impact where she lived, one and a half miles away.

This happened at about midnight and I was far from any major town or city. The pounding force had driven me all the way to the back corner of the sleeper berth of the cab. The cab and I were approximately three hundred feet from the main chassis. Parts and debris were spread a quarter mile down the very steep slope from the roadway to the final resting place. It took an eight man crew twelve hours to load all of the wreckage onto numerous flatbed trailers and haul it away.

Meanwhile, back to the accident, I was virtually pinned into the rear section of what remained of the cab. It had been compacted to about four and a half feet high. It took a special rescue operation to cut the corner of the cab roof to remove me from the twisted, mangled metal. They had to be very careful because there was over a hundred gallons of fuel spread out all around the area. I was trapped in the wreckage for over two hours and twenty minutes from the time of the wreck till I was removed and loaded into the EMS vehicle.

Photos on the following page show the extent of vehicle damage. The top photo shows the cab and the bottom photo shows cab chassis, which became separated during impact.

During this time I was conscious and talking to the rescue workers. There was one who could shine his light into a narrow opening and partially see me. My left foot was pinned up to the right side of my face. My left leg had a compound fracture of the femur and I could see the bone protruding through my jeans with a lot of blood. I could only move the fingers of my right hand and nothing else. The young man could reach in just enough to touch my arm. My forehead and scalp had several lacerations and I could feel the blood running over one eye and down my face.

The young worker kept trying to encourage me and said that the special saw and equipment would be there any minute now. He was somehow able to get a makeshift tourniquet on my leg to slow the bleeding. I could tell after a while by something in his voice that he was not completely convinced that I was going to get out of there alive. He touched me and began to pray and that made me more worried. Finally they were able to cut and peel the roof up. Then they cut the steel and other parts that had me pinned and lifted me out. As they began to put me on a portable gurney, one said "This is going to hurt so hold on." They gave my broken leg a sudden jerk to straighten it out. The pain was excruciating. Then they strapped me on that slab and with a cable, winched me up the steep embankment to the EMS vehicle. Then came the long and painful ride to the hospital which was thirty four miles away.

Chapter 21
THE AGONY OF THE ACCIDENT,
THE PLEASURE OF THE DRUGS
(GOD OR LUCK?)

After many x-rays and tests they finally gave me some pain medication. My leg was placed in traction for two weeks before they could do surgery and install rods and pins. They would daily change the sheets on my bed and I would always dread it. Although I was on heavy pain medication and they took extra care to slide the sheets from head to foot, they could not avoid the bones grating against each other with the slightest of movement.

My accident hit the local paper and the caption indicated that it was nothing short of a miracle that I was alive. My fiancee, her sister and brother-in-law made the ten hour drive that weekend to visit me. They also went to the yard where the wreckage was taken and took photos of the remains of the rig. Anyone, including fellow truckers, who ever saw these photos say that they cannot believe the driver lived.

There was this wonderful family that would come to visit patients at Butler County Memorial Hospital where I was. Their last name was Campbell and they were so kind and generous. They had read about me in the paper, I guess, and came to see me. They would always bring me brownies and snacks. The Mom would always have her Bible, and she and the three children would pray with me and tell me that Jesus kept me alive for a reason. They would come in at least twice a week because they knew that I had no family close by to visit with me. I was polite and cordial when they would come, but I couldn't wait for them to leave so that I could light up a cigarette. I just never felt comfortable smoking while they were there. They would always say "Jesus loves you" and that they would be praying for me. I never thought that God had saved me from dying in that truck, but that I was just lucky.

Finally the day came when they did the surgery on my femur. After regaining consciousness from the OR, I felt a deep burning pain in my leg like I had never felt in my life. They had made an incision in my left hip and screwed a fourteen inch threaded rod through the marrow of my femur, joining the break together. They kept telling me that all of my vital signs had to stabilize before they could give me anything for pain. Finally they gave me some medication and I felt some relief. My left knee was swollen twice its normal size since the accident, but they said it would go down.

Three days after the surgery they had me up and sitting in a large chair. The pain in my knee was excruciating, even with the medication. I kept telling them that something was wrong, but they said that it been x-rayed and everything was fine. After a few days I finally convinced them to take some x-rays of different angles or something. When they did, they found that the top half lobe of the tibia was fractured diagonally. They scheduled me for another surgery to install a pin in the tibia. This surgery involved the removal of the kneecap and drilling a ½" diameter hole straight through the tibia lobe, pulling the fractured section together with a threaded bolt-like pin with a rounded head on it. Then they reinstalled the kneecap and stitched up the skin to cover the bolt head.

When I came out of the OR, the pain was as bad, or worse than before. Again, I had to wait and suffer till they felt I was stable enough for the pain medication. Two days later, my leg was put into a soft cast from my ankle to my thigh. I remember that I would watch the clock for my shot. Five minutes before it was time for it, I would be pressing the button for the nurse to get there with it. Each injection began to leave a hard lump around it and the nurses were running out of places on my hips and buttocks. They could not give it in the shoulder muscle like with other shots. Well, my hips and bottom were covered with injection marks, but I still had to have it every four hours around the clock. All in all, I was hospitalized for fifty one days. That came to over three hundred shots. I remember the warm glow and the sensation of peace that I would get just after each shot.

Chapter 22
THE BONDAGE IS STRONG
CAUGHT IN THE NET

Being in there so long, I got to know everyone. A couple of the young nurses would sometimes come and visit with me after their shift. They would wheel me down to the outside to sit in the sun, and sometimes sneak me a couple of beers or sometimes smoke a little weed. The evening nurses would sometimes wonder why I was so happy when they came in on certain evenings. The Campbell family continued to visit and bring me snacks and treats till I left. I've always wanted to get in touch with them and tell them how much that meant to me, but I don't know how to.

Upon my release, I was given an unlimited prescription for Percodan and Darvocet. I began to experience the combination of alcohol and these other substances together. It was far better than alcohol alone. I was in a full leg cast from ankle to thigh and had to get used to using crutches. My Mom couldn't take care of me so I moved into my future in-laws' big farm house. Edgar, my future father-in-law and I, hit it off right away. He always kept at least one or two bottles of liquor in his pickup truck and he kept a limitless amount of #10 Valium and Nembutal, which is a very strong sleeping agent. We used to drink together quite a bit.

While in the hospital, I would complain about my left wrist swelling and being painful. The nurses said that it was because some of the IV needles had missed and it would soon get better.

I was assigned to an orthopedic specialist after being sent home to follow up on my recovery and physical therapy. I finally convinced him to take different angles of x-rays of my wrist because it was becoming increasingly more difficult to apply pressure to my left crutch grip. He found a small bone in my wrist that had completely split and shifted.

He said that there was very little that surgery could do at this point as it had been months since the accident. I still live with that, but it doesn't keep me from working and running a business. I remained on crutches for about seven months and fell a lot, especially out of Edgar's pickup truck.

Chapter 23
MARRIAGE DIDN'T CHANGE THINGS
VERY MUCH

My fiancee, who is the one who kept flirting with me at school, even when she was with her boy friend, chased me long enough that I finally quit running. Besides, I think in some twisted way, since my lost love hated her so much, I thought, she is the one I should marry. A lot of my friends said that she was not the one for me and that we didn't even make a good looking couple. Well, I didn't listen to them and married her anyway. We lived with her parents for awhile. Then we moved into a small rental house. We were always fighting because neither of us trusted the other and for good reason. We decided that since everyone knew her reputation, and mine was no better, that our surroundings and friends were a lot of the problem.

The brother of the semi truck owner had moved to Northwestern New Jersey. He had gone to work for his brother-in-law with a drywall supply business. They had a complete fleet of trucks and supplied drywall and building materials for new construction within about a hundred mile radius. When I spoke to Danny (the brother) he said that his brother-in-law was not happy with their mechanic and he had put in a good word for me. My wife and I decided that she would stay with her parents and I would move to

New Jersey and get a job. I was to live in a cheap hotel room and save enough money to get us an apartment. She would move up with our furniture later.

Well, I went to work for that company and continued drinking every night. I met Danny's sister, who was going through a divorce, and started seeing her. One night on the way to her house I was stopped for a routine traffic stop because I still had Virginia license plates. The officers started snooping around in my car and caught a glimpse of the stock of a gun mostly covered with a blanket. It was my twelve gauge shotgun, which was my companion. This did not go well in New Jersey. I was promptly cuffed and jailed in Washington, New Jersey. In NY State and NJ there is usually a mandatory sentence of one year for this offense. The next morning I got out of jail and called my boss. He called his attorney and six hundred dollars later all records were lost. I continued to work for the same company and was making good money. I got a room at an old three story hotel in Andover, NJ. It was just ten minutes from my work. The only problem was that there was a bar downstairs that stayed open till two a.m. I often went to work with a hangover.

I finally saved enough money to rent a brand new garden apartment and my wife moved up and brought our furniture. We lived there and fought there for about eighteen months. While we were there, her grandmother died. She had a big beautiful farmhouse on fifty-two acres with barns, sheds and all kinds of buildings.

I had only one more arrest while in NJ. I was busted for possession of illegal substances with intent to distribute. After making bail, we returned to Maryland and tried to start over there.

Chapter 24
THINGS GET PRETTY CRAZY

I went to work at one of the local auto dealerships. My brother-in-law, who worked for NASA and spent many evenings down at the club on base, came up with a great idea. He would finance it and we would be in partnership owning this gas station that sold beer and wine. I would run it during the day and he would run it a few hours in the evening. This was like turning the fox loose to watch the chickens. Now I was surrounded by booze with nobody overseeing me, and Edgar visiting me two or three times a day. It looked great at first, but sometimes my hangovers would cause me to open an hour or so late. The regulars didn't like this too much. You see, this wasn't just a package store. We had a bar with a pool table, etc. and the patrons liked to congregate there and drink. It wasn't one of those self-serve stations, I would have to pump their gas come rain or snow. When I got off work, I didn't always want to go straight home. In fact, I seldom did. I would sometimes stumble in at midnight or one o'clock and wonder why my wife was upset. It wasn't long before she started finding places to go too.

I hooked up with a friend named Eddie and started hanging out in some of the black clubs and neighborhoods. He knew everybody and got me into a lot of places that others couldn't. I occasionally got the evil eye from one of the crowd, but that didn't matter to me because I was probably a little crazier than he was. We started handling some pretty good drugs and getting in with some of the important people there.

One weekend Eddie and I had to make a little trip to score some stuff. We left Friday evening and by the time we got back and made the necessary drops, and of course, stopped at a few clubs, it was noon on Sunday. We rolled up into my yard and I went into the back door and into the kitchen. I was met with a lot of cursing, accusations, etc. I told her to shut up because I didn't have time for this right now.

I turned to get a glass from the cabinet and she swung as hard as she could with her fist. She caught me right in the side of my face and temple. I immediately punched her and she went flying across the kitchen. She got up and went out of the kitchen. I thought she had gone to the bathroom or to get an ice pack or something. The next thing I knew, she came charging in with my 25 caliber that I kept in the desk drawer in the hall. I always kept one piece in the car and one in the house. She was almost right to me when I realized what she had in her hand. She had intended to put it to my chest and fire because she wasn't a very good aim from a distance. When I saw what she was holding I smacked her arm to one side and the gun fired. The bullet just grazed the right side of my shirt near my ribs and went through the range door. I knocked the gun out of her hand and picked it up. By this time Eddie was out the door and I think in the next county! I just took the gun and grabbed some of my clothes. I went over to Eddie's for a while.

Chapter 25
HINDSIGHT

I can understand why God said "Do not commit adultery." When a spouse commits adultery, it causes the scorned one to despise the other to the point of killing them. In some twisted way, one can despise the person and yet, cannot stand to see them with someone else. I had known of some of her cheating on me and she knew of some of mine as well.

It is amazing how you can feel as though you can't live without someone and yet resent and despise them for what they have done, even when you have done the same wrong. I know there are many in prison today for life sentences for this very reason. They could never love that person, but could not stand to see them with another. It seems to happen much more when alcoholism and addiction are an issue. I heard someone once say that "An alcoholic doesn't form relationships, he takes hostages." How very true this statement is.

Well, my wife had endured enough and filed for a divorce. While we were married, she had even cheated on me with some of my so called friends.

After we separated, I remember some nights I would drive to the house where we lived together at about two or three o'clock in the morning and recognize a certain car parked outside. I knew they were in the house together and had often contemplated breaking in and killing them, but I would eventually drive off and sleep in my car.

Chapter 26
STIRRING THE INGREDIENTS

My brother-in-law and I were having a rough partnership as well as rough relationships, so we thought it best to dissolve the partnership. I began to stay at various places, wherever I could crash for the evening. I would hang out at one specific bar more than others and shot a lot of pool. One night as I was shooting pool, I noticed a girl that I had never seen there before. I caught her looking in my direction more than once. I had a few more drinks and got the courage to go over and sit next to her at the bar. I introduced myself and found out that she was from a town in Virginia about one hour south of us. She too was presently going through a divorce. We hit it off and started seeing each other. Before we knew it we had moved in together into a small apartment in Virginia.

I had been dealing in pot pretty heavily prior to meeting her. I felt that it gave me power to supply these people and a chance to get real friends who relied on me, since I was always very lonely by myself. There was one particular guy that bought several ounces at a time from me. I had known him for quite a while and always saw him at the party scenes. What my fellow dealers and I didn't know was that he had been busted in the next state, but things were kept pretty quiet. The authorities convinced him to work for them instead of doing a lot of time. We were at the Starlight Lounge (our favorite night spot) on a Friday night. The next thing we knew the band stopped playing and there were about twenty Feds rushing in and a few more at each entrance and exit with drug dogs. They came in with warrants and before it was over there were nineteen of us cuffed and on our way to jail. Each of us had multiple counts of selling to a narcotics agent. Well, I sat in jail till my hearing came up.

When court day came the only thing that kept me from going up the river was the fact that the now Deputy Sheriff was a former pal of mine who skipped school and partied with me when we were younger. He put in a good word to the judge for me and I got a three year suspended sentence with probation. The girl that I was living with really surprised me by coming to visit me often and waited for me to get out. She liked to smoke a little pot and pop a little speed, but was not much of a drinker at all.

After a while I started the same old routine, staying out late and getting very drunk. I started to get mean and more violent with my drinking. We began to have a lot of problems. She decided to move to a small town in South Jersey where her brother was living at the time. We had already found out that each of us had been unfaithful on one or two occasions. Well, there I was alone again and very lonely in an old two bedroom one bath mobile home. She did not give me the location or phone number where she would be in Jersey. This was to be a trial separation, but I suspected that it was more than that. Her parents were some of those "born again" Christians and they wanted her to get her life together. That meant getting me out of it.

After about a month, I did some investigating and questioned some people. I found out where she was living and decided to give her a surprise visit. Maybe we could work things out. When I got to the home where her brother lived he said that she wasn't there right now and pointed to a house a few doors down where she might be. Instead of surprising her I was the one in for a surprise. No one answered the door, so I went in. I didn't see anyone downstairs so I went upstairs.

Much to my surprise she was in bed with another guy getting high and having a good time. She knew with my temper what I was about to do to him, so she wrapped herself in a sheet and started crying. She asked me to please come downstairs and talk. I agreed, at least for now, to not do any surgery on him. I wanted to see what she had to say. She gave me this story of how much she missed me and that she had gotten really wasted that day on cocaine, pot and liquor and didn't know what she was doing. She said that if I agreed not to hurt him she would leave with me. We could stay with her brother and try to make things work between us and I was just lonely and dumb enough to try it.

She was working a small local pub at night and I got a job at the local Ford Dealership. I had a friend in Maryland with a pickup truck and he helped me move my large tool cabinets and tools to my new job. Things seemed to go pretty smoothly for a short time, but every time I would see that other guy (he was a small time local dealer) in the bar or I would get real drunk, I would throw that incident up to her and we would end up fighting. We started jumping around from one apartment to another after the rent got overdue.

Chapter 27
MISSING BROTHER

My oldest brother, John, moved up from Maryland to stay with us for a while. He found a job in a small town called Port Norris, NJ. He stayed with us and saved some money to move to Florida. He had no car and hitchhiked everywhere he went. He left my apartment in October 1978 in Millville, NJ. He was supposed to be going to Florida and had a moderate sum of cash with him.

Our family has never seen or heard from him since that day, though we have tried many avenues to find him. His full name is Elwood John Harris, Jr. and he was born on July 26th, 1944. My greatest prayer is that my Mother, who is now eighty-one years old, could see her eldest child once more before she leaves this earth. It has been twenty-eight years since we have seen him. We all love and miss him.

Chapter 28
RIDE THE MERRY GO ROUND

I finally got fired from the Ford place because of my attitude and lack of attendance. I was beginning to rely on alcohol now for everything. I remember keeping a bottle of liquor and a glass of ice in the freezer. I sometimes would awake at three a.m. with the shakes. I would try to quietly go into the kitchen and put water in the glass of ice. I would then try to get a shot of liquor down me and chase it with the ice cold water to keep it down. If the first one didn't work, I was right next to the sink for it to come back up. It got to the point where I would set the alarm an hour before my girlfriend had to get up and go down to make some coffee. I would pretend to be in the kitchen drinking coffee and getting ready for work. I was really trying to get at least three shots in me to stop the shaking, so that by the time she came down I was more steady.

I was driving an old '66 Plymouth Valiant with a broken windshield and crushed hood and fender. The floors were rotted out in places so you could see the road passing under you as you drove. I would keep a half-pint bottle of booze under the seat and every morning just before arriving to work I would pull in behind this small strip mall. I would get a couple more shots to stay down and proceed to go to work as if everything was fine. Some days I was just so very sick that I couldn't make it in to work. When I was at work, as soon as I had a car ready to road test, I would go to the package store drive thru and get a couple of beers to calm my nerves. I would quickly gulp them down and toss the bottles out into the ditch.

One night my girlfriend awoke with severe abdominal pains and went to the doctor in the morning. He did some tests and confirmed that she had cysts on her ovaries and would require surgery very soon. They also concluded that they would probably have to do a hysterectomy at the same time. I woke up very early on the morning of her surgery. I went through my usual morning ritual and was somewhat calm when she came downstairs. We only had one car running at the time so I would have to drive to the hospital and then go to work.

She pleaded with me to call in to work and stay with her at the hospital as she was very scared and anxious. I told her that if I missed anymore days I probably would be fired and there were some jobs I had to finish since I was the one who dismantled them. Well, I dropped her off at the OR walk-in and drove off. As the sun came up, I decided that it was too nice a day to go to work and I was feeling pretty badly at the time. I waited till five minutes after eight and called in to work. I explained to my boss about the surgery and that I felt I should be with her. He said he understood and that I should be with her. She was only twenty-six at this time and the surgery was pretty serious and permanent as far as she was concerned.

After getting off the phone, I went to the closest pub and ordered a draught beer and a shot of brandy. I kept on drinking from place to place that day. As five o'clock approached I figured that I'd better get to the hospital around five thirty so it would appear that I had just gotten off work. When I walked in she was crying hysterically and the nurses were trying to calm her. When she looked at me all I could see in her eyes was hurt and hatred. Little did I know that when she came out of the OR and the anesthesia wore off, she called my work twice to talk to me. The second time she called they told her that I called in and never showed up for work. Needless to say, by the look I got from her and the nurses, I was not feeling very proud of myself. After she cursed me and screamed at me a few times I turned and left.

I proceed to get even drunker than before. The terrible twisted idea of alcohol to an alcoholic is that the very substance that made you sick and ashamed is the only substance you can trust to help you forget and feel better again. It's like a merry-go-round that keeps spinning you deeper and deeper and you can't get off. I have known alcoholics that were told by doctors that their liver could never handle them drinking again and that they would die if they did so. After some period of abstinence it seemed the compulsion and fears would come upon them and the feeling of helplessness and compulsion would override what the doctors had told them. They would again begin drinking and surely died.

I, myself, was dying of alcoholism at the age of twenty-nine and could not bring myself to face that truth. I could not imagine life without alcohol. It seemed to be the glue that held me together and the only thing I could trust to do for me what I needed. Nobody knows what I'm expressing here unless you have experienced it for yourself.

Chapter 29
DESPERATE MEASURES

The job that I had after being fired from the Ford Dealership was working for a very large produce farmer. They raised many crops and had their own refrigerated food storage semi trucks and all kinds of equipment. Alcohol had such a hold on me that I kept half-pint bottles up in the parts loft, sometimes stuffed in parts and boxes. I sometimes had to go into town to parts suppliers to pick up parts. I had designated road culverts and places where I had hidden bottles along the route. I would simply pull over as if checking a tire or something and grab the bottle from under a rock, gulp down a few shots and chase it with Sprite or water. This was my last job before going into treatment. After the surgery incident things were never the same with us.

One day I was really down and called my brother-in-law in Maryland. I knew he was a recovering alcoholic and I was hoping he could tell me what to do. What he told me I didn't really want to hear. He said that I needed to find a detox center or recovery center and check myself in. I didn't like that at all. Things were getting so bad at home, I thought that if I showed some effort in trying to get help that she might give me another chance. I checked myself into a county run detox center in Salem, NJ. It was an old renovated three-story house with seven bedrooms. She took me there and stayed till I filled out all the forms, and then she left me there. I had tried to drink a few shots on the way, I figured it would be a while before I had anymore.

Just prior to seeking help.

I was not assigned a bedroom but had to sleep on an old army cot next to the office. They had to monitor me for the next forty-eight to seventy-two hours in case I had seizures or something. I had also been mixing the drinking with Percodan and Tylenol III with codeine. I spent the next five days on that cot only getting up to run to the bathroom to throw up or get a drink of water. I thought I was going to die. I would sweat profusely and then I would tremble with chills. There was severe burning up my spine and the back of my head felt like it was going to explode at times. My body hurt in places that I didn't even know existed. I couldn't sleep more than ten minutes at a time and

I'd wake up trembling and sweating. The desk clerk and nurse would occasionally stop by and tell me that I was going to get better. This went on day and night. All I could think about was where my girlfriend was and what she was doing. She never called to check on me.

After about six days I was able to keep down some soup and crackers.

After seven days it was mandated that you had to attend a Twelve Step meeting that was next door. I had to attend a ten a.m. meeting and return again at seven p.m. I hated those meetings because people were saying that they could never drink again and I felt that they were trying to get me to talk too. After nine days I finally reached my girlfriend at home and told her that I was all better and asked her to please come get me. I packed and left against the advice of the counselor and staff.

Chapter 30
HERE WE GO AGAIN

After getting home I didn't drink for a couple of days, but then I got a bright idea. I told her that they had taught us that we could learn how to control our drinking by only having a couple and keeping a log record of them. She knew nothing of the Twelve Step Program, so she bought it. We went to the local pub and I think I had a couple of mugs of beer and she had a mixed drink. I went home very proud of myself. Within a very short time I was telling her that I was going somewhere for a job. I was stopping into my old spots having a few drinks. I was very careful not to come home drunk because after all, "I had learned to master this thing."

Well, we now had two cars again, even though they had Virginia tags and no insurance. As I was headed home one evening, I noticed our other car at a pub we used to frequent before my stay at the center. I stopped and went into the dimly lit bar. I didn't see her at the pool tables or bar so I walked back to the booths and there she was sitting with another guy. He had his arm around her affectionately and they just happened to kiss as I walked up. When she saw me her face turned white and so did his. I don't have to tell you what happened next. I went ballistic and a lot of things took place. She managed to get to the apartment, grab some of her clothes and get away as quickly as she could.

For the next few days I stayed in the apartment with the blinds closed and just drank myself into oblivion. There was a package store within walking distance. That was the only place I left the apartment for. I remember sometimes waking up, looking at the clock and not knowing if it was six a.m. or six p.m. I lost all track of time and I wasn't eating either. I began to see things that I don't think were really there. Sometimes I would wake up on the living room floor or the kitchen floor and didn't remember lying down there. Fear began to grip me and I kept all the lights on in the apartment. I would take my gun and look under the bed and in the closets because I thought I saw a strange person at the top of the stairs at times. I received a notice stating that the power would be cut off due to lack of payment. The landlord left a note on the door about my two months back rent and that I had to get out.

I wasn't doing any more pills, but I was only drinking Black Velvet whiskey. I had run out of money for booze and had to taper off a little. I walked by the kitchen table and saw the phone book already open to the page with the detox number circled. I never knew where the phone book was so that seemed very strange to me. At least the phone had not been cut off yet so I called the number.

I knew that if they would take me back I wouldn't have to sleep in my car. I would have a roof over my head, heat and food for at least twenty-eight days. It was October and getting cold in NJ. Marsha answered my call. She was the only one out of all of them who had been nice and compassionate to me before. She said that they only had one opening and if I promised to show up she would hold it for me. I threw my clothes in the old car and that's the last thing I remember till I was sitting at the desk in Salem signing in, again. They told me the next morning that I drove right into their backyard, parked my car and came right in instead of parking out front by the curb. I don't remember one part of the forty minute drive there.

Chapter 31
WORKING THE SYSTEM

After a couple of days on the cot and being under observation, they felt that I could be assigned to the only bed open at the time. I was on the third floor in the back of the house. I soon won the trust of the staff and could go to the Post Office to get the mail with another person. Soon I was permitted to walk alone to the local market to get snacks and go to the Post Office.

There was a bar and package store just down the block from the market. I would stop in and get a pint or half pint of Vodka which I thought could not be detected by smell as much as other liquors. I would also get breath mints. I'd come in the front door with the bags of snacks that the other patients ordered and go straight upstairs to distribute them to their respective rooms. As I was doing this, I would quickly slip the bottle into my room and under the mattress. As soon as I finished handing out the snacks I would tie a string to the neck of the bottle and hang it outside my window. I knew that there would be unannounced searches of the rooms for drugs and alcohol. The staff would check in the toilet tanks as well. They never suspected a bottle attached to a string outside the window. I would wait till everyone was watching TV and pretend to go to my room to read. I drank just enough to get a good buzz but not enough to cause suspicion.

After twenty-nine days in the seven day detox center a bed became available in a county funded rehab center, about a one hour drive from where I was. I drove myself there, stopping early on my journey to buy a half pint of Vodka. I made sure that I had plenty of breath mints on hand. I drank the whole bottle on the way just as they expected me to. Since the place was far out in the country, I said that I got lost a couple of times. The staff accepted that excuse and we proceed with the orientation. I was admitted and assigned a bunk in one of the small cabins. It was to be a twenty-eight day program of recovery. I did not like the sessions where they would try to get you to express your feelings or to find out was going on inside you.

I had no intentions of staying sober. In September or October of 1978 I was taken to a local physician from the detox center. He filled out a form for me to collect unemployment disability. The diagnosis was classified as 'chronic alcoholism.' I was awaiting approval and expecting several weeks of back compensation to come in as one big check. Then I would leave there as fast as I could.

Meanwhile I continued to go to all the meetings and sessions, which were mandatory. While I was there three patients were caught smoking pot which had been smuggled in by a visitor. All three were asked to leave that day. I remember that one young man was pleading to stay, since it would violate his parole and he would return to jail. There was a small, frail girl named Dorothy who had been forced into prostitution because of her habit. She also pleaded that they not force her to leave. They were all three kicked out that afternoon.

We learned three days later that Dorothy was found in a cheap motel room near Atlantic City. She had either hanged herself or had some assistance. Some of the other patients that had gotten to know her wept and we had a special meeting for everyone to express their thoughts or feelings. I never really got to know her, so I figured that this meant there was one less hooker on the streets.

While I was there I never got an opportunity to get anything to drink. There was a female patient there who was about as happy to be there as I was. She was a card dealer and part time hooker at one of the casinos in Atlantic City. We kind of hit it off but there were no male/female relations allowed at the center. We both agreed to borrow a little money from some of our fellow patients and planned our exit. We were able to get a few dollars together and took off for Atlantic City. My first stop was for gas and a twelve pack of beer to start the trip. We made the three hour drive, stopping to get liquor and beer. When we arrived at her sister's apartment, she didn't seem too thrilled to see her out of rehab, especially being accompanied by me. We stayed there a couple of days drinking and getting high. Finally, out of money, she decided to check herself into another place for help.

Chapter 32
A TOUCH OF NORMAL

I still had not gotten my expected unemployment check, so I was back out on the street. I decided to check into the Atlantic City Detox Center to wait out the process. While there, one of the counselors mentioned a halfway house in Carney's Point, NJ. She knew the director very well and convinced him to interview me for possible admittance. The director's name was Bill H. and for some reason I found favor with him at our first meeting. I was taken back to the detox center where my car was and the counselor gave me ten dollars for gas to drive back to Carney's Point. I put six dollars worth of gas in the tank and bought a half-pint of Vodka and a pack of breath mints. It was about a three-and-a-half to four hour drive and I drank the bottle and made sure I had plenty of breath mints before my arrival.

I was assigned a bunk on the second floor of an old three story farmhouse that was owned by a local doctor who was also in the Twelve Step Program. The facility housed about ten men and the director also had his own room there. He was a retired union spokesman for Dupont, about seventy years of age. He had his own place and owned a duplex in Woodstown. He seldom drove himself but had one of the licensed men from the facility take him wherever he needed to go. Somehow I became his personal driver in a short time. I would take him to the grocery store, post office and bank. Everyone registered at the home had to sign up for food stamps. I remember how embarrassed I was standing in the line waiting my turn for an interview. I was approved and had my photo card issued that day.

January 1979 while in halfway house. Photo from old food stamp card.

Bill, the director, had a lot of business friends in the area. He arranged for an interview for me with the owner of the local Ford-Lincoln-Mercury dealer. Just before I was hired I received my check from unemployment disability in the amount of fourteen hundred dollars for all the back pay owed to me. The car I was driving was a wreck, I don't know how I got anywhere with it. Bill knew a retired doctor that was selling a very nice Buick that was only eight years old. We went to look at it and it was like new. Bill took me to his bank, co-signed my check and I opened a checking account. I then went and purchased the Buick. I was hired at the dealership and began to work regularly as I stayed at the halfway house. After a couple of months, one side of Bill's duplex became available and he rented it to me for a very reasonable price. He almost seemed like a father to me. I would go to Twelve Step meetings with him, driving his car as he insisted. I would also spend many evenings at the halfway house watching TV and hanging out with him. There was a young man that was there even before I got there. His name was Jimmy and I could sense that he had a lot of jealousy and hatred towards me. He thought that he was Bill's favorite before I came along. I think his mind had been damaged to some degree due to his drug use from the time he was eleven years old. One evening I was sitting on the sofa watching TV with Bill who was in his recliner. There was another young man there named Chris. I saw Jimmy coming in from the kitchen door with a butcher knife in his hand. He was walking straight toward Bill saying "I'm going to kill you." I jumped up and faced him. He slashed at me saying "I'm going to do you first."

He had no idea just how many sharp objects I had previously been attacked with. Chris, who was much bigger than Jimmy, grabbed him from behind and held him in a full nelson headlock. He began to spit at me and growl like a dog. After getting the knife away from him we strapped him in a wooden chair while Bill called 911.

When the two large men came in they easily subdued him and put a straight jacket on him. He was still spitting at me, growling and saying "I'm going to kill you." He had apparently smuggled in some liquor and drugs that day and was very much out of his mind. They hauled him off somewhere and I never saw him again.

After that incident Bill treated me more like a son than before. I could ask him for anything and he would do his best to do it.

I had a good job, good friends, a nice apartment and car, the only thing that could make it perfect was to be able to go out and have a couple of beers like others did. Occasionally I would drive to the next town where no one knew me and have a couple mugs of beer and shoot a game or two of pool. This worked for a while and I was able to keep Bill completely in the dark. In the meantime at my workplace, it took only four months for me to be promoted to Service Manager. I seemed to have everyone fooled and was really able to drink socially and not go to extreme.

Chapter 33
FREEDOM ON THE HORIZON
THE BEGINNING OF THE END

One Friday evening I took a customer's Lincoln home with me to try to diagnose a vibration and noise complaint. I told the owner and he agreed. After I got a shower and dressed I decided to go to a small pub and have a beer and shoot some pool. While there I thought I should go over to Vineland to visit my Hispanic neighborhood friends and show off the Lincoln. When I arrived at the home of one of my old associates he was just on his way out to a party. He suggested I follow him over and join them. I had a few beers at the party and decided to head to Atlantic City to a casino. The next thing I recall is waking up with cars blowing their horns as they attempted to pass me. I was sitting still in the fast lane of Rt. 40, a four lane highway, heading west. The car was running and the headlights were on but I was just sitting there. I was startled by the horns and began to proceed with the traffic trying to get my bearings on where I was.

After seeing the road sign for 40 West, I knew I was heading towards home. I looked at the clock in the dash and it said 2:15 a.m. I don't recall anything after leaving the Vineyard party at 9:30 p.m. As I drove towards home, I began to shiver and shake. All of the things that I had ever done wrong were replaying in my head. I tried to shake it off and finish the bottle of beer I had between my legs. I felt a dark depression and despair come over me. It was as if something was telling me "It is hopeless, you are hopeless." I felt that even the Twelve Step Program would not work for me as it had for others. I had been going to meetings and saw others getting better. Again, as I drove on, everything I had done wrong was playing in my head.

When I finally reached my apartment I was still shaking. I went in and fell on my knees beside the bed and cried out "God if you are real and you are everything they say you are, then please take this craving and compulsion to drink away from me forever. I don't want it anymore." Tears were rolling down my face as I prayed sincerely. I recall brief prayers when I would get into trouble, but this was different in a very real way. I rolled into bed and either fell asleep or passed out.

I got up Saturday around noon and went out see Bill. From there I went to a meeting. I continued going to them regularly and getting involved. Bill never knew about my setbacks. He asked me to speak at a very large hospital speaker's meeting with two others in Wilmington, Delaware. I reluctantly said okay because I didn't want to disappoint him. We were each to speak for about fifteen minutes of our drinking and recovery. I was so nervous that my knees were knocking and trembling, but I made it through. Bill told me on the way home that he was very proud of me. I don't remember anyone ever saying that before.

One afternoon I was walking down the street, I looked to my left, and there was a pub that I used to frequent. I looked across the street corner and there was another one. There seemed to be a voice inside me saying "You can go into either one of those" and I said "Yes I can, but I don't want to." Just then I remembered my prayer on July 15th, 1979 beside my bed. It had been five months and I had not had a drink, nor did I have a compulsion to do so. Then it seemed as though a light bulb came on inside my head and I remembered what I prayed for.

I prayed "God if you are real, take this craving and compulsion to drink away from me forever, I'm sick of it!" I've never had a drink since then. Some may say it was coincidental or your willpower got stronger. To them I would say, "After all the jails, detox centers, rehab, halfway house and loved ones trying to help me, nothing worked for me till I earnestly asked Him to take it away."

I know in my heart that something supernatural happened that night I prayed to be set free from this compulsive bondage. It seems that where before I had no ability or power to make a choice, I could now choose wisely, and not surrender to it.

PART II
FREEDOM

Chapter 34
A DIFFERENT DIRECTION, DIFFERENT WAYS

I continued to work and go to Twelve Step meetings. I also spent a lot of time with my sponsor, Bill, and hung out at the halfway house a lot when I was off work. I guess the only thing I never shared with Bill was how God had set me free from alcohol. You see, he had been sober for about seven years but he never wanted to hear about God or any religion. He had a mouth on him like a drunken sailor whether he was in the presence of women or men. He was also not above taking advantage of some newer females that came into the program. He did not smoke because he had lung cancer three years prior and had a lung removed.

My oldest sister had recently moved to southwest Florida with her husband and two daughters. I drove down one weekend to visit my Mom in Maryland and she was so happy to see me sober and doing so well. We talked about taking a vacation and driving to Florida to visit my sister, since my Mom had never been there. When I returned to work the next week I spoke to my boss and asked if I could drive my new Mercury demo when we went. He said that would be fine. My Mom and I made plans to make the trip in February after speaking to my sister. When February arrived I packed my things, drove to Maryland to pick up Mom and we drove to Florida. I remember when we left Maryland it was freezing rain and by the time we got to Florida it was in the mid eighties. Mom was like a child seeing all the orange groves and palm trees for the first time. We spent about five days at my sister's and got to see a lot of sights there.

I attended some Twelve Step meetings while there to try to meet some new people. I happened to mention to a man named Jerry that I was a mechanic and currently was service manager at a dealership. It just so happened that he owned a repair shop and would soon have an opening for a good mechanic. He told me that if I decided to move down, please mail a resume with references and he would take me on. Before Mom and I left we had made a decision to move down there. We talked about it on the way home and made some tentative plans.

When I returned to work I gave my boss a ninety day notice. That would give him plenty of time to fill my position. In the meantime my brother Bob with his girlfriend and my sister Sandy with her fiancee, who all lived in North Carolina, decided to move to Florida with us. Well, three months later we had all moved into one house about thirty minutes from my sister Charlotte. I went to work for Jerry and the others started looking for jobs. My Mom and I had sold a lot of our possessions and put our money together into a joint account. After about two months and not finding a job, my brother decided to go back to North Carolina. About four months later, Sandy's fiancee joined the Air Force and was stationed in North Dakota. She moved back to Carolina with my sister Kathy while her fiancee was in boot camp.

After a short time I could tell that it was not working out with Jerry and I. We had a disagreement and he fired me. I began putting in applications and checking the classifieds.

I had gotten a sponsor named Hal in the Twelve Step Program (a sponsor in the Twelve Step Program is simply a mentor to confide in and form a relationship with). I had done some work on Hal's vehicles and he asked me "Why don't you go to work for yourself?"

The thought of not having a guaranteed income each week and working for myself scared me, especially since I knew so few people in the area. When I picked up my last paycheck from Jerry I noticed that it was a lot less than I expected. He claimed that a certain job I did came back and had to be corrected. He decided to deduct from my check the amount that he claimed it required to fix the problem. This was preposterous and illegal since I was being paid by the hour and not by the job. I left there upset and called Hal to talk to him. He told me that even though Jerry had cheated me I had to forgive him and pray for him. At first I argued with him but decided to follow his instructions since they aligned with the steps of the program.

One of the first things I learned after getting into the Twelve Step Program was that holding resentments was one of the fastest ways to start drinking again. Well, I prayed for God to help me forgive Jerry and asked God to bless him.

Chapter 35
TRYING IT GOD'S WAY

As I mentioned before, Mom and I had closed out our accounts and put everything into a joint account when we moved to Florida. With five people living in the house and I the only one employed, we had just about exhausted our resources. Not that my brother and sister and the others had not tried to find work, they had tried many places. I found myself unemployed and the utility bills and rent were almost due and there weren't enough funds to cover them. As I was discussing this with Hal, he reminded me that I had made a decision to turn my will and life over to God, as it says in Step Three of my program. He also asked if I was still praying for Jerry and had forgiven him. I replied "Yes" and decided to just trust and believe that God had not brought me this far to leave me and my mother homeless.

The next day a series of unusual events began to unfold. A check came in the mail for Mom in the amount of five hundred dollars. Her bank in Maryland had sent it to her with the explanation that she had failed to enter a five hundred dollar deposit some time ago and they had just discovered it. The next day she received a check from her former propane gas dealer in the amount of two hundred-ninety dollars. They said that she had made an overpayment and they were refunding that to her. We checked all of her old checkbooks and past records and found no such errors on her part. I also began getting phone calls from strangers asking if I could come out and fix their cars.

I had a camper shell on the back of my El Camino so I packed several of my tools and small tool cabinets in the back and turned it into a service vehicle. Within thirty days I was getting jobs on a daily basis. My Mom also got a few upscale homes to clean weekly and things started looking up. I often wondered that if I had not forgiven Jerry and not begun trusting <u>totally</u> in God, if these things would have come about.

This was the second event that I had recognized as God's intervention in my life when I needed Him most. It wasn't long before I was thanking God for getting fired and making a lot more money. I don't think I would have ever gotten the confidence or courage to 'step out of the boat,' so to speak, without 'having the rug pulled out from under me.'

Chapter 36
12 STEP PROGRAM HAS AN IMPACT

I know now that God had everything under control because I never placed an ad anywhere and yet my work continued to increase. My sponsor, Hal, was very involved in area service with the Twelve Step Program and I too started becoming involved. My first involvement was to become a GSR, short for General Service Representative, for a specific group meeting. I enjoyed traveling to different conferences and conventions all over South Florida on the weekends. We would stay at very nice hotels and convention centers. We attended workshops and other meetings as well as made a lot of new friends. It helped me a lot in getting over the fear of speaking in front of a group. Hal's wife and several others in our area were also involved and would attend these functions as well.

In the Twelve Step Program and living in South Florida, 1981.

There was one gentleman named Ed who was in his early sixties. His wife was very ill and required an in-home nurse. He had children and grandchildren and been had sober for about fifteen years. I attended many meetings with him but he never liked to speak about God.

When we all attended these conferences we usually shared rooms and split the expenses, which made it easier on everyone. On one particular weekend I shared a room with Ed. On arriving late Friday night, we all got settled into our rooms and met down in the lobby for coffee and registration. We also signed up for certain Saturday workshops. We then went out as a group for a late dinner and fellowship. Saturday went very well with meetings, lunch, and later a speaker's meeting and dinner.

As I was preparing for bed, Ed was sitting in a chair watching me while the TV was on. He said "I really like looking at young muscular men with nice tans." I just looked at him kind of strange. Then he asked "Would you completely disrobe for me, I just want to look at you?" I let him know in no uncertain terms where I stood on that issue. I also told him that if he had any intentions of laying a hand on me, he would not look the same when he left as when he came here.

That was the last discussion we ever had on that subject. I must admit that I was more than a little shocked and surprised with Ed, though. He had very little to say to me when we crossed paths after that incident.

I was elected DCM, short for District Committee Member. Their responsibility is to stay in contact with the GSR of several groups and attend those group's meetings to see if there is any way we can help them or turn in any suggestions to the district committee on how things could be done better (this is in no way a complete description of the responsibilities of the GSR or DCM). I was later elected Treatment Facility Chairman for District Five and was heavily involved in the jails and treatment facility meetings in our area.

Chapter 37
DOES IT ALWAYS HAVE TO BE THIS WAY?

There were a few meetings where it was regular practice to go out in a small group for coffee and dessert to a local restaurant. There was a lady named Claire who would frequent these small gatherings. One evening she mentioned that her daughter Vicki, who was twenty-three, was moving here from Houston in a few weeks. She said that she was beautiful and she wanted us to meet. When Vicki arrived and got settled in, Claire invited me over for dinner to meet her. When I got there and we were introduced my heart started pounding like a drum.

I pretended to be cool and all together but inside I was a nervous wreck. I had never had anyone with her looks even give me the time of day, let alone actually carry on a conversation with me. The evening went well, we enjoyed dinner and I said goodnight. I didn't want to seem over anxious so I waited till the second day to call Claire. I pretended to call and thank her for dinner then casually asked if Vicki was there. When she came to the phone and said hello I got a lump in my throat. I tried to seem together and confident by just asking if she had gotten out the day before to see any of the sights. She said that she had not really gotten out much yet. I then asked her if I could show her around that evening and maybe get something to eat. When she said yes I almost dropped the phone, but regained my composure.

That evening we went for a walk in Gilcrest Park next to the river. We sat on a park bench and talked about a lot of things. About the only things I was used to talking about lately were the program, my past and sobriety. I was kind of shocked when she seemed genuinely interested in what I had to say. She even shared some things that happened in her childhood and how she used to get drunk to escape, but she didn't drink anymore. I don't remember if we even went to eat that night, I just remember walking, talking and looking up at the stars. I didn't tell her that it was my Mom's car I was driving because all I had was an old panel truck that was my service vehicle after the El Camino.

We started seeing each other more often but I kept wondering why she was seeing me when she could have anybody in the whole world if she wanted to. After we were together for a couple of months I thought I should ask her to marry me before she woke up and realized that I wasn't exactly a prize catch. What shocked me even more was that when I asked her she said yes. We set a date and had the Justice of the Peace perform the ceremony with a small family group at my sister Charlotte's home.

I continued working as usual and she got a job at an upscale waterfront restaurant. She worked the night shift serving alcohol and food. She mentioned on one occasion that her boss had tried to make advances at her as he had also done to other girls there, even though he was married with two young children. He liked to buy the employees drinks and hang around after closing time, thinking he was a real ladies man.

Vicki never drank any alcohol while we were going together, but after going to work there she began to stay after her shift and have a drink or two with the other employees. When this first started she would get home before midnight, but gradually she started getting in later. She said that her co-workers and boss would sometimes go to one of the other late night bars. She also said that it was harmless and she had let her boss know in no uncertain terms where she stood. But I could not accept or understand why she continued to go out after work. On one occasion her boss apparently said something to another man at the other bar and got a nice black eye out of it. He was even barred from the place since it catered to a more upscale clientele. Vicki was eventually getting in at two a.m. or later. It almost seemed like I was reaping what I had sown in my prior relationships. I began to know the feeling of jealousy and distrust that they must have felt with me.

We began to have a lot of disagreements, although not loud. I asked her to please find a different job, working days, but she insisted that she would never make nearly as much money. She began to keep wine in the refrigerator and order wine or a drink when we went out to eat. As the nights got longer and her return home got later I began to feel jealous, angry, and not very needed. After five months of marriage and more and more arguing, she suggested that maybe we had made a mistake by getting married. She said that she missed all of her friends in Houston and wanted to move back there. I suggested that we seek counseling and try to work things out but she was pretty convinced that it wouldn't help. I felt helpless, rejected, angry and hurt. It seemed that the very things that I feared before the marriage were coming true. I would never let her know that she could hurt me and pretended to go along with the dissolving of the marriage and let her go. I still could not figure out what had happened and why she changed so much. I found myself asking God why He let this happen, especially since I wasn't drinking any more and was doing everything I could to help others get sober and stay sober.

I felt angry and let down by God, since we had begun our marriage by praying together every morning and every night. I would find myself sitting on the park bench next to the river at sunset crying out to God and asking Him "Why?" I felt very depressed and did not want to work. The only things that seemed to help were getting more deeply involved in helping others in the program and avoiding being alone.

Chapter 38
GOD HAS A WAY

Even though I prayed, I wanted nothing to do with Christianity or the Bible. I remember chairing a meeting one night in Englewood, where a young man brought a Bible with him. During the meeting he began referring to certain scriptures and I became very annoyed with him. I asked him to take his Bible back out to his car, as it had nothing to do with our Twelve Step Program. God began to place more and more Christians in my path and kept telling me that if I didn't accept His son Jesus, that I couldn't know the Father either. I continued to reject these Christians and convinced myself that they were no better than the ones I had known in my childhood.

I began to frequent a family owned Italian restaurant since I didn't like to cook and eat alone at home. I met a waitress named Paula who waited on me often. She was currently in a somewhat broken relationship. I asked her out to dinner, she accepted, and we saw each other maybe two or three times. I sensed that there was not much there between us. One evening as she was waiting my table I saw a very beautiful young girl waiting on another table some distance away. I casually asked Paula if she was a new employee since I didn't remember seeing her there before. I didn't want to seem overly interested so I didn't ask her name. Strangely enough, Paula said her name was Bonnie, and she had been working there for a short time.

The next time I went in I asked the hostess/owner to please seat me in Bonnie's section. She smiled as if she knew something was up since we both knew that Paula was off that night. I didn't show any interest towards Bonnie, I just ordered my food. I began to ask for Bonnie's section each time I went in and stopped asking Paula out. One evening as she finished waiting on me and brought me my check, I asked her if she was seeing anyone (at least this is the way I recall it). She said no and it was either that evening or my next visit to the restaurant that I asked if she would go out with me. She invited me to join her at a church social dinner. As much as I wanted to go out with her, I found an excuse not to make it.

I was not prepared to set my foot in a church or to get involved with a church group. She told me that she had a little girl who was two years old, and she finally agreed to accompany me to the beach on her day off with her daughter, Brandi. I finally agreed to meet some of her friends from church at a Wednesday night fellowship at a home and not a church. I didn't know at the time that it was her

Pastor's home. They seemed very warm and friendly when we arrived. He played the guitar and they sang some songs. They served refreshments and we just talked about different things. A small group of us was sitting in the living room when an older man named Riley looked at me and said "I believe God wants to heal your back and spine." He asked if I was having spinal problems or any pain. I was having severe low back pain and had been seeing a chiropractor three times a week and was not getting any relief. Riley caught me quite off guard and I stared at him wondering how he knew about my pain since I never mentioned it. He said that he believed that God would heal me and asked if they could pray for me right then and there. My head was spinning with thoughts of how he knew this but I didn't want to embarrass myself in front of Bonnie. I said that it would be okay for them to pray for me. They had no idea that the x-rays from the doctor showed that my left leg was one half inch shorter than my right leg due to the severe accident and botched femur surgery. The chiropractor said that the difference in leg lengths was causing my pelvis to throw off the alignment of the lower spine, causing the pain. I was sitting in a folding chair in the Pastor's living room, when he knelt down and lifted my legs up. He placed my feet in each of his palms as three or four others stood behind me. He was not holding or pulling on either foot and it was obvious to me and everyone else that the left leg was shorter. As they began to lay hands on my shoulders, head and spine, they began to pray in Jesus' name and began to praise Him. I felt an unusual warmth, much like a heating pad, on my left hip, lower back and left thigh. I didn't pray or even close my eyes, but began to feel something like muscle spasms in the same warm areas.

As I sat there in amazement, I watched my left leg grow out beyond the right and then equal to the right. When they stopped praying one of them told me to stand up and try to touch my toes. I stood and not only touched my toes, but could place my palms flat on the floor with no pain. I didn't know what to say or what had just happened, I just knew that there was no more pain. They all began praising and giving thanks to Jesus. After the fellowship I said thank you and goodbye.

PART III
VICTORY

Chapter 39
LETTING GO AND TRUSTING GOD

I could hardly go to sleep that night for thinking about what had happened to me. As I mentioned earlier, God continued to send Christians in my path. One of them was a gentleman in his late fifties named Barney. He was in the Twelve Step Program with me and I saw him at all of the Agape conferences and retreats. He always seemed to have such peace and joy and usually had a small circle of people he talked with. I had gotten to know him casually and knew that he had about thirteen years of sobriety. When I shared with him my incident of healing, he smiled and said "Sit down here and let me share something with you." He began by telling me of an event in his life that happened about eight years prior. He said that during his search for God in the Twelve Steps, that he had visited a Wednesday night service at a church in Fort Meyers. After the service was over he was walking to his car when a man called him over to where he and three others were standing and asked if they could pray for him. The man said that God had told him that Barney had diabetes and that He wanted to heal him. Barney said that he could not how that man knew this. He was taking insulin shots daily and had to watch everything he ate very closely. As these men prayed for him, he felt an unusual feeling going through his body and sensed that he was being healed. He told me that he has never had to take another insulin shot and could eat anything he wanted. He hugged me and said that Jesus is the only way to God. Whenever I prayed, I never really knew if God heard me or even cared.

A couple of weeks later I went to visit Barney at Fort Meyers Beach where he lived at a marina on a large boat that he owned. I spent a couple of days hanging out and talking with him. On Wednesday night I agreed to accompany him to his church in Fort Meyers. It was called Love and Grace Fellowship with Dr. Bill Besansky as pastor. After the service the pastor asked if anyone wanted to come to Jesus and give their heart to Him. I went down front and prayed "Lord Jesus, I believe you died for my sins and the sins of all men. I believed that you were raised from the dead to give me eternal life. I give my heart to you. Come and be my Lord and Savior." I was taken to a side room and they laid hands on me for the Baptism in the Holy Spirit and explained to me what it meant to be filled with the Holy Spirit. They also told me what it was to be 'Born Again.' I left and went back to the boat with Barney, we prayed and rejoiced together. That night I slept like a baby and had peace like I had never known. After leaving Barney, I went back home. I had to know more about this God who really heals and really loves and really answers prayers.

Bonnie and all of her church family were thrilled to hear that I gave my heart and life to Jesus.

They told me that about being baptized in water and shortly thereafter we were all gathered at a brother's house for a covered dish dinner. The pastor said anyone who wanted to be water baptized should get into the swimming pool and I got baptized right then and there.

Bonnie shared a story with me about how Jesus had healed her daughter Brandi. When Brandi was very young, whenever she got a fever or ear infection, she would often have a seizure. Her eyes would roll back and her breathing would change. Bonnie had gotten Born Again and had gotten into a true Bible believing church. She had learned through the word of God that she nor Brandi had to tolerate sickness anymore because it is written that "By His stripes we were healed!" One day shortly after Bonnie was saved, Brandi came down with the same old symptoms. Bonnie had no car so she had a friend drive her to the ER. On the way she remembered what she had learned. As Brandi laid in her lap having a seizure, she laid hands on her and said "Satan, I bind you in the name of Jesus, you will take your hands off her and never return because the word says that by His stripes we were healed." Bonnie said that immediately Brandi's eyes refocused, her breathing became normal and when they arrived at the ER, they could find nothing wrong with her. She is now twenty-four years old with a three year old daughter of her own and I can tell you that she never had another seizure since that day Bonnie stood on God's word.

I began to share Jesus with others. I started reading the Bible to find out all I could about this God that I had never known before. I took two young men that were in the program aside (their names were Jeff and Pat) and shared Jesus with them. They came to our church and received Jesus as I had. The first miracle I remember after my being saved was right after their salvation. They too had heard the word of healing. I had five warts that had appeared on my hands. Two years prior to this the doctor had burned four from my left hand and five from my right hand. I could not work on cars or put my hands into any chemical for at least two weeks until they healed. Jeff and Pat were at my apartment one afternoon and I asked them to pray over my hands for the warts to disappear and not return. In two days all of the warts were gone leaving no scars. That was twenty one years ago and I haven't had another wart since.

I was sponsoring an elderly gentleman in the program. He was about seventy years old and had completed the twenty-eight day rehab center. He had been sober for six months. I asked him to help me set up and co-chair a meeting for a month. On the day of the meeting he called me at four thirty p.m. and said that he was having a migraine headache and would be unable to help me that day. I asked him if he wanted me to pray for him. He said yes, so I spoke the healing word over him and told him to expect to see a change very soon. He called me back in twenty minutes and sounded like a kid who had just gotten a new bike. He said as soon as we got off the phone earlier, the pain started to ease off and now it was gone completely. He said that before it always made him nauseous and would put him into bed for hours. He said that he couldn't wait to get to the meeting and help me. He was totally amazed that God could heal him through a telephone conversation. He shared this with many and got some amazing responses and, also, some strange responses.

Chapter 40
THAT WHICH GOD HAS JOINED

Getting back to Bonnie and me, we dated for awhile and I asked her to marry me. She said yes so we set the date for June 1st. We just had a small gathering at the church with my sister Charlotte and some of our church family. Our pastor performed the ceremony and we had a small reception at our home.

We went to Cancun for five days while our pastor and his wife kept Brandi. Then we picked her up and went to Disney World for three days. I'll never forget how Brandi always wanted to keep her Mom all to herself. Whenever we would sit on the sofa together, Brandi would always squeeze between us and hug her Mom. She didn't like the idea of me moving in on her territory, but later on she became a Daddy's girl. She would go to the mall with me and we did many things together. I still remember teaching her to ride a bike. I eventually became Dad.

Bonnie and me at our wedding reception June 1, 1985.

It was very tough for me that first year or two because I had never been a parent and knew nothing on the subject. I sometimes felt that I was being pulled in too many directions. I was trying to learn to be a Christian husband, a Christian father, a Christian businessman, and I was also still involved in the program. I remember many times jumping into the car and racing over to our pastor's home and just ranting and raving about things that we were going through. Instead of arguing with me, Bonnie learned early that it was more fruitful to go to her Heavenly Father and ask Him to straighten me out or to open my eyes. It would always work because I would feel a conviction or an inner knowing that I had to change something. Of course, that didn't always stop my stubbornness. We had some ups and downs that first year or two, but I can honestly say that we have never raised a hand to one another.

We gained a great deal of wisdom from our pastors, Jim and Veronica, about what it meant to be in a covenant which was bound by a promise and not by emotions. I can't put into words what it means to know that you can trust your spouse to be faithful, even when you don't agree on everything. We have truly grown together over the years and I can say with great confidence that she is faithful, steadfast, strong, loving, patient and trustworthy. It is because of these qualities that I have come to love her more than anyone that has ever been in my life. She has been patient and forgiving even when it has taken me a long time to learn something or to accept it.

Chapter 41
THE VICTORY
GOD'S MIRACLE WORKING POWER

Stepping back just a little, when Brandi was ten years old, Bonnie gave birth to our daughter and we named her Madeline. We had a midwife and a home birth. We had friends singing and praising the Lord as Madeline came forth into this world.

We knew we would have a healthy baby because when we first learned that we had conceived, we had our pastor's wife lay hands on Bonnie's abdomen. Our pastor, his wife, Bonnie and I bound the enemy from coming near that child and spoke the word of protection about her. I have heard many people question why some parents have healthy babies and others do not. The Lord showed me that he always creates perfect things, but it is Satan who comes to steal, kill and destroy.

Many people have to realize that the baby is a baby and a new life at the time of conception and not nine months later when it is seen. During that period is when Satan comes and perverts God's creation. Even most Christians are ignorant of this. God created music, sex, TV, the weather and many other things that Satan has snuck in and perverted, and so it is very important for anyone who has conceived a child to have true believers to anoint you and bind the enemy. You are to let him know that "in the Name of Jesus" this child is off limits to him. Then continue to sing hymns and speak Psalms and the word of God concerning His covenant and healing wholeness promises daily over that new life. We are not ignorant of his devices.

I recall a night when Madeline was very small. She woke us up crying loudly at about one a.m. I felt her and she was burning up with fever. I picked her up, held her in my arms and walked back and forth. The first thing I said was "How dare you Satan try to come against this precious one that is under our covering and covenant." I said "You will leave her now in the name of Jesus because it is written that surely He bore our diseases, illnesses and pain and by His stripes, we are healed." Within minutes the fever was gone and Madeline slept like an angel.

We had a single mother with three children start coming to our church. The church was helping her in every way that we could. One day she called Bonnie and asked if she could please drop off her kids at our house and have Bonnie watch them while she went to the doctor or somewhere. Bonnie agreed and they spent the afternoon there playing with Madeline who was almost two years old now. Later the mom came and got them. Around two a.m. Madeline woke us up screaming. When Bonnie went to pick her up she would not allow her to. She was always so close to Bonnie that it seemed like the cord had never been cut. Well I recognized in the spirit that there was more to this than could be seen. I forcefully picked up Madeline and she kicked at me, screaming. I pulled her close to me and I said "In the name of Jesus, you foul spirit get out of here. You have no place here because this is the temple of the Holy Spirit that you are trespassing on." In seconds Madeline became very calm and reached out for Bonnie to take her. Bonnie held and comforted her.

When Brandi was thirteen years old she spent the night at a friend's house. Her father was the caretaker of a very wealthy man's ranch. They had a vehicle that they called "the gator." It had no top but you could drive it all over the ranch. The girls were not supposed to be in it but the other girl was driving it pretty fast and heading straight for a tree. Brandi was able to bail out just before hitting the tree and landed on her ankle. There was immediate pain and swelling. The girl and her dad rushed Brandi to the ER. It was Saturday and my pastor and I were building a new sound booth in our church. When they took some x-rays they found a fracture in the bone just above the ankle. There was no orthopedic specialist there on the weekends, so they put on a soft cast and made an appointment for Monday with the orthopedic specialist. As soon as they left the ER Brandi insisted they take her over to the church where we were working and have us pray for her instead of taking her home first. My pastor and I anointed her and spoke the written word of God over her and believed that she was healed, even though it was swollen twice the size of her other ankle.

Monday the swelling had gone when she went to the specialist. He took more x-rays and compared them to the ER's x-rays which showed a defined fracture. He said that he could not explain it but the fracture and swelling were gone. He could find nothing wrong with her ankle. Praise God!

Chapter 42
LEARNING GOD'S WAYS, SPIRITUAL LAWS

One of the first revelations I had after being saved was the law of sowing and reaping. A short time after Bonnie and I met, she shared with me that she didn't have a car and had to get rides from church members to work and back when she was first saved. She was renting a house with another young Christian single mom and shared the rent and expenses each month. She was just getting by, paying the babysitter and going to the store to buy a big box of cereal and some of those "four for a dollar" frozen pot pies. She would give Brandi a bowl of cereal in the morning and she got lunch at her babysitter's house. Bonnie would heat a pot pie for Brandi's dinner and eat only what was left when Brandi was done. That was her dinner and things were very tight. She told me how she had gotten the revelation of sowing seed into the Kingdom. She began to tithe, even though it looked like she couldn't afford it, in the natural.

As she became obedient to the Word, she noticed something happening. When the rent and bills were due and she needed a specific amount of money to meet those needs, she would get exactly that amount along with enough to pay the babysitter. Many times her tips, at that time, would be exactly what she needed, to the penny. It happened week after week, to the point that it could not have been coincidental. She needed a car and one day she heard of a need where a sister in the Lord had a small sum of money stolen from her at work. The Lord impressed upon Bonnie's heart to give her seven times the amount of that which was stolen, even though she could not afford it in the natural. A day or two following her obedience, she was blessed with a car that was worth more than ten times what she had sown. It seemed that God was going out of His way to prove Himself true to His word. When I heard these things I began to be stirred in my Spirit.

When I had taken Bonnie on that first date to the beach, I had to borrow my land lady's car because all I had to drive was my old service truck. Even though I was working steady, I wasn't able to save enough money to get a car and I had no credit to finance one. I began to take God at His word and started to tithe weekly. Not long after that I bought a cassette tape of a group called Petra. For those younger readers, a cassette tape was the recording after the eight track and before the CD. Anyway, I listened to the music and I took out the cardboard insert that listed the lyrics and info about the group's members. As I read through it, one of the guys was endorsing a missionary organization called Compassion International. He shared how he began by sponsoring one child and now he was sponsoring three or four. I believe there was a photo of him with one of these children and I had a strong urge to get involved. I began sponsoring a little boy in Mexico before Bonnie and I married. Not long after that I had the opportunity to buy a small sports car for very little money, because it wasn't running and needed some work. I fixed the problems and got it running. One of my female customers saw the car and asked me how much I would sell it for. She had a very nice Oldsmobile Cutlass Supreme and offered to trade it for the sports car. She had just gotten divorced and wanted to make her ex-husband jealous by having this car. We made the trade and I had a very nice, clean, practical car for my new family.

Bonnie and I continued tithing as one and continued to seek God's direction on other outreaches and ministries that He wanted us to support. We would pray and if both of us had peace about it we would do so.

I had built a sort of dune buggy/street buggy that was not very practical at all. At the end of our street was a large enclosed walk-in van for sale. Several times we passed by it and Bonnie would suggest to stop and ask how much he wanted for it, as it was the perfect vehicle to carry all my tools, welders, air equipment, etc. All these things would not fit into my pick up truck. Well men, I'm here to tell you that sometimes, make that many times, we need to listen to what our wives have to say and truly seek God together on issues. I had been trying to sell that old buggy for eighteen hundred dollars and been very unsuccessful. I finally stopped to inquire about this large van. It just so happened that he was asking eighteen hundred dollars for it. I was reluctant to stop before because I was sure that he would want much more than that. He seemed very interested in my buggy and came to my house and drove it. We immediately made an even trade. Bonnie did not let me forget that for weeks. Listen to your wife! I was able to put four times the equipment in the van than I could in my truck. It helped me to have everything I needed on service calls instead of having to drive back and forth. As a result, I became more productive and increased my income.

Chapter 43
MORE GLORY FOR THE LORD

At this time we were renting a small older two bedroom/two bath house and we opened it on Wednesday nights for home fellowship. We had a group leader and his wife and baby son who came faithfully each week. They would come early and set up the playpen for the baby in our living room. We had some wonderful anointed teachings and ministry there. We had the desire to buy our own home but had no credit. Not bad credit, but no credit. We even applied for a Sears charge card after we were married and were turned down. We continued to tithe and watch for opportunities that God would put in our path to sow seeds and began to reap abundantly because God's word <u>never</u> fails.

We were praying for a home when a young lady started coming to our church. She was in the real estate business and happened to mention to us that there was a very nice home only a short distance from where we currently lived. The sellers were going through a divorce and were motivated to sell quickly. We went to look at the home and loved it. The only financial references that I had were the auto parts stores and our utility companies. We filled out all of the applications for the loan and prayed to God for a supernatural favor in this situation. When we applied, the mortgage interest rate was 9.75%.

After a few weeks we got a response from the financial board, saying they needed proof of our income. We got my financial statements together, as the mortgage rate dropped to 9.25%. We sent what they requested and awaited their response. Later we got another letter stating that they needed more information. The interest rate continued to drop as we kept sending them the information they requested. If it were up to me, I would have closed on the house when the rate was at its highest, but God had a better plan. Finally when the rate went down to a low point of 8.5%, we were approved and closed on the house. The difference in what we would have paid in interest was thousands of dollars. That's Covenant prices! That's my Father's way of doing things, even though my anxiousness would have cost us much more. God began to prosper us so that we could buy new furniture for our new home instead of buying things on credit and paying much more for financing. He began to teach us to be good stewards of what He was entrusting us with.

Although I was still not advertising in any way, my work continued to increase to the point of having to get a shop with lifts. I was becoming more productive not spending time working mobile, running from job to job, and running for parts. Within one year I had to double my shop and hire help to get the work done. Bonnie was teaching K5 at a Christian School and God continued to bless us more and more. It seems that my Father can't wait to bless our obedience when we are in line with His word.

Chapter 44
GOD CONTINUES TO BE IN CHARGE

After many years in South Florida, many of our close friends who were biological family within themselves and like family to us, moved to Eastern Tennessee. We prayed and sought God's direction and also expressed our desire to move to the mountains and experience the four seasons (especially spring and fall). I flew up there from Florida to check on commercial properties as well as homes. Within a few months we were loading the moving truck and heading north.

We settled in a beautiful neighborhood with a twelve month lease so that we could get acquainted with building contractors, etc. We bought some commercial property and built a large building. The Lord sent us customers three weeks prior to our opening date. We now have a full service automotive center to make any major or minor repairs on import or domestic vehicles. We also have a huge showroom that Bonnie manages which is filled with all types of accessories for trucks, SUVs and cars. God has blessed and prospered us far above we were doing in Florida. There are many whom God sends to our showroom to be ministered to or prayed for, not just for auto repairs or accessories.

Since we have come to understand the scripture in Matthew 6:33, which says, "Seek ye first the kingdom of God, and all these things will be added unto you," meaning all the things we need to function in this world, we have been blessed beyond anything we could have ever imagined. We are now able to give away (sow) more than I used to make. We have a nice home in the country with a beautiful view of the Smoky Mountains from our deck and front porch. I often stand and stare at God's wonderful creation from our yard.

There are many Christians who don't understand covenant. Once you make the covenant, and truly understand whom you have made the covenant with, you will understand that it is much like the covenant that you have made with your spouse. When I married Bonnie everything that I had became hers, and everything that was hers became mine as well. There was no more 'mine and yours.' The same thing is true with my Heavenly Father. One can have all the wealth in the world as long as it does not have them. My Father loves to bless us so that we can spill over on others and help finance the Gospel all over the world.

I once heard about a woman who was the housekeeper of a very wealthy man. While he was living he gave her a beautiful manila envelope with a large photo of himself and some pretty papers inside. He did not know that she could not read or write. When he died she moved out of the mansion and began living on the street. She kept her possessions in an old burlap bag. She was very proud of the photo of her former employer and often showed it to others. When she finally died penniless someone went through her bag. In there was his last will and testament. He had left his entire estate, including the mansion, to her. Yet she lived as a beggar because she did not know what was legally and rightfully hers. Many Christians today are the same as that lady. They lose out because they can't truly understand their covenant with the Creator of all things and they never have anything to give to others or to finance the Gospel. This is not God's will for His covenant children!

Since I have given my heart to Jesus I have seen my brother Bob and my sisters, Charlotte, Linda, Kathy, Sandy, and April ask Jesus into their hearts. They all say that they saw such a miraculous change in my life, that it had to be God and nothing else. They have not all followed up and become all that God wants them to be yet, but I am believing with all my whole heart that before Jesus returns (and that being soon), that He finds them doing His will.

Bonnie and I are continuing to grow in the Lord and together. I have said many times that my Christian walk has reflected all the grace of a pregnant giraffe. Even though this may be true, I refuse to give up or go back from where I came. If I had to point to anyone besides the Holy Spirit that has caused me to grow, it would be my beautiful, youthful, loving, determined, very intelligent and patient bride Bonnie. Don't ever buy into that notion that there is such a thing as a 'marriage made in Heaven.' We have made our marriage here and understand together what our covenant with God means and what our covenant with each other means. If we live only by our emotions Satan will dominate us. God has established that we are to dominate Satan and all his demons. Jesus won this for us already. We are to occupy till His return.

Chapter 45
KNOWING GOD WELL ENOUGH
TO BE COMFORTABLE IN HIS PRESENCE

U nlike my earthly father, my Heavenly Father welcomes me into His presence. I can sit on His lap and remind Him of His word, as He has told us to do. I can share my deepest thoughts and desires without being slapped down and rejected.

Jesus said "When you have seen me, you have seen the Father." Jesus never denied anyone healing and He is the same yesterday, today and forever, as it says in Hebrews 13. He loves to heal. All it takes is to take Him at His word and speak it with the authority He has given us in Jesus' name. We speak what He says in His word about it.

Chapter46
OTHERS WHO TRULY FOLLOW THE LIVING GOD

Last year I went to visit my family members in North Carolina. My sister Linda along with my niece, nephew and his friend were walking out into the parking lot from the superstore. I noticed that Linda was limping and I asked her what was wrong with her. She said that her doctor had determined from x-rays that she had a heel spur and that in the mornings she could not bear any weight on her foot.

As we approached her car, I asked her to sit in the driver's seat with her legs out of the door. I crouched down, and holding her foot and leg, began to speak the Word of healing over her while the kids bounced around the car. There were people walking by wondering what I was doing.

The Lord touched her that day and she says that she has not had the pain since. If I had to remember and list all the miracles that the Lord has performed in the last twenty-one years of my life, it would make this book so large that no one could pick it up for its sheer volume and weight.

I often say that Bonnie is like a pit bull when it comes to believing. Once she sinks her teeth into the situation and begins speaking the word, in faith, she stays locked onto it till it lines up and conforms to His word. We felt urged by the Lord for her to begin taking flying lessons and become a pilot. She has been obedient to that and is very close to getting her pilot's license. Flying can be an expensive "hobby" but where God gives vison he makes provision. She wanted to be a good steward and had prayed that she wasn't being foolish in spending so much on lessons. About two weeks later a man named Doug, whom we go to church with approached Bonnie. He is a Chaplin at Fort Sanders Hospital in Knoxville. He asked her if she had thought about flying. She told him yes and that she only had a few hours of training so far. He said that he owned a Cessna airplane and that God had put her on his heart to use his plane. He said God impressed on his hearts to sow it as seed because God wanted to train a missionary. We are now believing Him for a plane of our own and know God will provide when the time is right.

I am not a person who flatters someone but I believe in honoring those who are being obedient to their calling. There is a precious man of God named John and his wife Doris. Over sixteen years ago we met them in Florida. They had just returned from a mission trip to Kenya. He had retired earlier that year as a Structural Engineer. They did not retire, but refired, and now head up a powerful ministry called Missionaries in Action. We felt led to partner with them and have done so for the last sixteen years. John just turned eighty-one years young. He and Doris have established many churches and have raised up many pastors. They have also established sewing factories to take women off the streets and teach them a trade and skill. They make clothing and become an asset to the community, but more importantly, become daughters of the Living God. I told John recently that he is an inspiration to me because of his faithfulness. When the Lord returns I want to be doing as John and Doris are.

I will never endorse a ministry or outreach unless I have a personal knowledge of the fruit they are bearing and have a witness in my spirit to hook up with them. Some of these ministries are: Missionaries in Action in Kenya, Missions Impossible in Haiti, Compassion International in Colorado Springs, Colorado, Joyce Meyer Ministries, Ken Copeland Ministries, Jesse Duplantis Ministries, Chuck Colson Ministries, Benny Hinn Ministries, World Challenge headed by David Wilkerson in NY, Karen Wheaton Ministries, Trinity Broadcast Network, Billie Brim Ministries, Mac and Lynn Hammond Ministries and John Hagee Ministries. These are men and women of God who have laid their lives down to touch the lives of precious children and families all over the world. They know what it means to be ambassadors for Christ (2 Corinthians 5:20) and walk in the authority that Jesus gave us (Luke 10:19). They are also not intimidated by Satan's smokescreens and deceptions (Phil 2:10). They know that greater is He that is in them than he that is in the world. They know that God created man in His image and gave him dominion and that Satan can never have dominion because he was not born here (Genesis 1:26-28).

They truly understand the scripture that says "When you have done it unto the least of these, you have done it unto me." Jesus said that! When you partner with these, every life that is touched and every soul that is saved is accounted to you as if you were there yourself. The only question that should be on your mind is when you stand before the Lord, will He say "Well done, good and faithful servant, enter into my rest?" I pray that it will be so in your life.

Chapter 47
MY CHOICE

At the time that I am writing this I have been blessed with 27 years of sobriety and I am free from substance abuse as well. It really is difficult to put into words the difference between the despair and hopelessness of my life 27 years ago and how meaningful, and wonderful my life is now. I can only say it seems like the difference, in my vision of, what hell and heaven are like in my finite mind.

I thank God everyday, that I am not tempted, nor even desire to drink again. I also thank Him for the ability to choose right thinking and not having to be a puppet to negative feelings and events. That is true victory and freedom over all bondage!

Chapter 48
YOUR CHOICE

Please remember that God really loves you no matter who you are, no matter what your past. God loves you so much that He sent His only Son for you. Jesus laid down His life and rose again so that we could spend eternity in Heaven and experience His absolute best here on earth. If you would like to know this life, say the following prayer and mean it from your heart.

"Heavenly Father, I admit that I am a sinner. Right now I choose to turn away from sin. I ask you to cleanse me from all unrighteousness. I believe that your Son, Jesus, died on the cross to take away my sins. I believe that He rose again from the dead so that I might be forgiven of my sins and made righteous through faith in Him. I ask you, Jesus, to be the Savior and Lord of my life. Jesus, I choose to follow you and ask you to fill me with the power of your Holy Spirit. I declare right now that I am your child. I am free from sin and full of the righteousness of God. I am saved in Jesus' name. Amen."

The Bible says in John 3:16 "Whoever believes in Him shall not perish but have eternal life."